# AN INTRODUCTION TO PSYCHOLOGY

# AN INTRODUCTION TO PSYCHOLOGY

By

**WILHELM WUNDT**

TRANSLATED FROM THE SECOND GERMAN EDITION

By

**RUDOLF PINTNER,** M.A. (EDIN.), PH.D. (LEIPSIC)

GYAN

*Published by*

Gyan Publishing House
5, Ansari Road
Daryaganj, New Delhi-110002
Phone: 011-47034999, 9811692060
E-mail: books@gyanbooks.com

*Distribution Network*
gyanbooks.com
India, USA, Canada, UK, Australia, France



ISBN : 978-81-212-6492-1 (PB)
First Published, 1912

2nd Impression 2022

*Printed at:* Gyan Press, Delhi.



**AN INTRODUCTION TO PSYCHOLOGY**
Author: WILHELM WUNDT

# AN INTRODUCTION TO PSYCHOLOGY

BY

WILHELM WUNDT

PROFESSOR OF PHILOSOPHY IN THE UNIVERSITY OF LEIPSIC

TRANSLATED FROM THE SECOND GERMAN EDITION

BY

RUDOLF PINTNER, M.A. (EDIN.), PH.D. (LEIPSIC)

*Publication of the*
*"Pädagogische Literatur Gesellschaft Neue Bahnen"*

# AUTHOR'S PREFACE

It is not the intention of this introduction to psychology to discuss the scientific or philosophical conceptions of psychology, or even to make a survey of the investigations and their results. What this little book attempts is rather to introduce the reader to the principal thoughts underlying present-day experimental psychology, leaving out many facts and methods which would be necessary for a thorough study of the subject. To omit all mention of experimental methods and their results is at the present day impossible. Yet we only need to consider a comparatively small number of results of the first importance in order to comprehend the basal principles of the new psychology. To characterise the methods of this psychology it would be impossible to omit all reference to experiments, but we can and will omit reference to the more or less complicated instruments on which the carrying out of such experiments depends. I must refer the reader who wishes a fuller account of the new psychology to my *Outlines of Psychology*, which also contains the necessary bibliography of the subject.

W. WUNDT.

LEIPSIC, *June* 1911.

# TRANSLATOR'S NOTE

The present volume is a popular introduction to the Wundtian psychology. It is a shorter and simpler sketch than the same author's *Outlines of Psychology*, and it should prove invaluable to the English-speaking student who wishes to gain some conception of the subject before entering upon a deeper study of the same. Its popularity in Germany has been phenomenal.

In translating the work the translator has, as far as possible, used the same English terms as those employed in the translations of Wundt by Judd and Titchener.

He is greatly indebted to Mr. Robert Wilson, M.A., B.Sc., for his advice and help in reading over the manuscript before going to press.

RUDOLF PINTNER.

EDINBURGH, *May* 1912.

# CONTENTS

## CHAPTER I

### CONSCIOUSNESS AND ATTENTION



## CHAPTER II

### THE ELEMENTS OF CONSCIOUSNESS

## CHAPTER III

### ASSOCIATION



## CHAPTER IV

### APPERCEPTION

## CHAPTER V

### THE LAWS OF PSYCHICAL LIFE

# AN INTRODUCTION TO PSYCHOLOGY

## CHAPTER I

### CONSCIOUSNESS AND ATTENTION

If psychologists are asked, what the business of psychology is, they generally make some such answer as follows, if they belong to the empirical school: that this science has to investigate the facts of consciousness, its combinations and relations, so that it may ultimately discover the laws which govern these relations and combinations.

Now although this definition seems quite perfect, it is really to some extent a vicious circle. For if we ask further, what is this consciousness which psychology investigates? the answer will be, "It consists of the sum total of facts of which we are conscious." In spite of this, our definition is the simplest, and therefore for the present it will be well for us to keep to it. All objects of experience have this peculiarity, namely, that we cannot really define them but only point to them, and if they are of a complex nature analyse them into their separate qualities. Such an analysis we call a description. We will therefore best be able to answer more accurately the question as to the nature of psychology by describing as exactly as possible all the separate qualities of that consciousness, the content of which psychological investigation has to deal with.

For this purpose let us make use of a little instrument to help us—an instrument well known to all who have studied music, *i.e.* the metronome. It is really nothing more than a clockwork with an upright standing pendulum, on which a sliding weight is attached, so that beats may follow each other at equal intervals in greater or less rapidity. If the weight is fixed at the upper end of the pendulum, the beats follow each other at an interval of two seconds; if at the lower end, the interval is shortened to about a third of a second. Between these limits every different length of beat can be produced. We can, however, increase these limits considerably by taking off the sliding weight altogether. Now the lower limit falls to a quarter of a second. Similarly we can obtain any longer time we choose with a sufficient degree of accuracy, if we have some one to help us. Instead of letting the pendulum swing of its own accord, the assistant moves it backwards and forwards with his hand, measuring off the longer interval fixed upon, by means of a watch, that marks the seconds. This instrument is not only very useful for teaching singing and music, but it is also a psychological apparatus of the simplest kind. In psychology, as we shall see, we can use it for so many purposes that we are almost justified in saying that with its help we can demonstrate the most important part of the psychology of consciousness. In order to be able to do this the instrument must satisfy one requirement, which every instrument does not possess. The strength of the beats must be sufficiently uniform, so that even to the most attentive listener differences in the intensity of the successive beats may not be noticed. To test an instrument in this respect, we proceed thus. We subjectively emphasise the one beat and then the other, as the two following rows of notes show :—

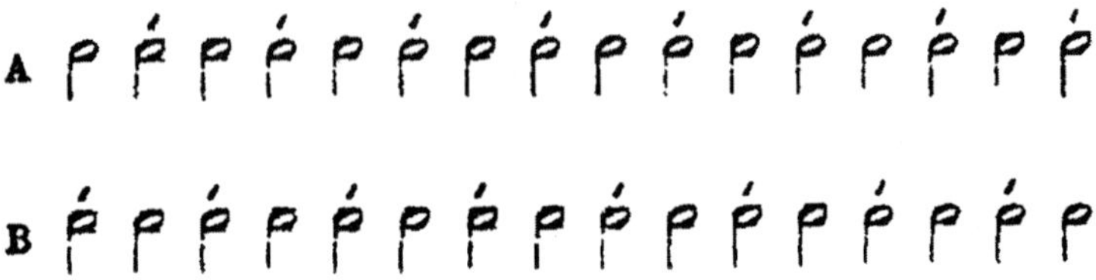

This diagram represents the separate beats by notes, and the accent shows those beats that are subjectively emphasised. Row A shows an ascending beat, and row B a descending one. Now if it happens that we can at will hear into the beats of the metronome an ascending or a descending beat (A or B), *i.e.* we can hear one and the same beat now emphasised and now unemphasised, then we may regard the instrument as suitable for all the psychological experiments to be described in the following pages.

Although the experiment described was only meant to serve as a test for the metronome, yet we can derive from it a remarkable psychological result. For we notice in this experiment that it is really extraordinarily difficult to hear the beats in absolutely the same intensity, or, to put it in other words, to hear unrhythmically. Again and again we recur to the ascending or descending beat. We can express this phenomenon in this sentence: Our consciousness is rhythmically disposed. The reason of this scarcely lies in a specific quality, peculiar to consciousness alone, but it clearly stands in the closest relationship to our whole psycho-physical organisation. Consciousness is rhythmically disposed, because the whole organism is rhythmically disposed. The movements of the heart, of breathing, of walking, take place rhythmically. In a normal state we certainly are not aware of the pulsations of the heart, but we do feel the movements of breathing, and they act upon us as very weak stimuli. Above all, the movements of walking form a very clear and recognisable background to our consciousness. Now our means of locomotion are in a certain sense natural pendulums, the movements of which generally follow with a certain regularity, as with the pendulum of the metronome. Therefore whenever we receive impressions in consciousness at similar stated intervals, we arrange them in a rhythmical form similar to that of our own outward movements. The special form of rhythm, ascending or descending, is within certain limits left to our own free choice, just as with the movements of locomotion, which may take the form of walking, of running, of jumping, and lastly of all different kinds of dances. Our consciousness is not a thing separated from our whole physical and mental being, but a collection of the contents that are most important for the mental side of this being.

We can obtain a further result from the experiment with the metronome described above, if we change the length of the ascending or descending row of beats. In our diagram each row, A and B, contains sixteen separate beats, or, taking one rise and fall together, eight double beats. If we listen attentively to a row of beats of this length when the metronome is going at a medium rapidity of, say, 1 to 1½ seconds, and then after a short pause repeat a row of exactly the same length, we recognise immediately the identity of the two. In the same way a difference will be immediately noticed, if the second row is only by one beat longer or shorter than the first. It is immaterial whether we beat in ascending or descending rhythm. Now it is obvious that such an immediate recognition of the identity of two successive rows is only possible if each of them is in consciousness as a whole. It is not at all necessary for both of them to be in consciousness at the same time. We can see at once that consciousness must grasp them as wholes, if we consider for one moment an analogous case, *e.g.* the recognition of a complex visual image. If we look, for example, at a regular hexagon for a short time, and then cast another glance at the same figure, we recognise at once that both images are identical. Such a recognition is impossible if we divide the figure up into several parts and show these parts separately. Just as the two visual images appeared in consciousness as wholes, so must each of our rows of beats appear as a whole, if the second is to call up a similar impression to the first. The difference consists in this, that the hexagon was perceived in all its parts at once, whereas the beats followed each other in succession. Just because they follow in this way, such a row of beats possesses this advantage, that we can thereby determine precisely how far we can extend such a row so that it is still possible to grasp it in consciousness as a whole. It has been proved by such experiments that sixteen successive beats, alternately rising and falling, or so-called $\frac{2}{8}$ time, is the maximum for such a row, in order that all the separate elements may still find room in our consciousness. We may therefore consider such a row as a measure for the scope of consciousness under these given conditions. At the same time it appears that this measure is, between certain limits, independent of the rapidity of succession of the beats. A grasping together of the row as a whole becomes, however, impossible, when the beats follow each other so slowly that no rhythm may be heard, or when the rapidity is so great that the $\frac{2}{8}$ time is lost, and the mind tries to group the beats together in a more complicated rhythm. The former limit lies at about $2\frac{1}{2}$ seconds, and the latter at 1 second.

When we take the longest row of beats that can be grasped together as one whole in consciousness under the given conditions and call this the scope of consciousness, it is of course obvious that we do not mean by this expression the total content of consciousness that is present at one given moment. We mean only to denote the maximum scope of one single complex whole. Let us picture consciousness for a moment as a plane surface of a limited extension. Then our scope of consciousness is one diameter of this surface, and not the whole extent. There may at the same time be many other elements of consciousness scattered about beside the ones we are just measuring. They can, however, in general be left out of account, since in a case such as ours consciousness will be directed to the content that is being measured, and the elements outside of this will be unclear, fluctuating, and isolated.

The scope of consciousness, in accordance with our definition, is a relatively constant value, if we keep to a special time, *e.g.* the $\frac{2}{8}$ time. It does not change with a different rapidity of beat within the above-mentioned limits. A change in the time, however, exercises great influence. Such a change is to some extent dependent upon our will. We can hear into our uniform row of beats not only a simple $\frac{2}{8}$ time, but a more complicated rhythm, *e.g.* the following $\frac{4}{4}$ time:—

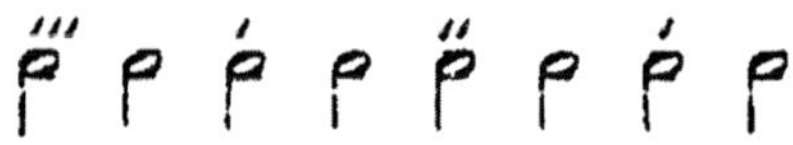

Such a row arises if we let different intensities of accent enter, say the strongest at the beginning of the row, a medium one in the middle, and a weak one in the middle of each of the two halves of the whole row, as in the diagram above. The strongest emphasis is denoted by three accents, the medium one by two, and the weak ones by one. This transition to more complicated rhythms is to a great degree dependent upon the rapidity of the beat, as well as upon our will. With long intervals it is very difficult to go beyond the simple $\frac{2}{8}$ time. With short ones a certain exertion is necessary to withstand the impulse of transition to more complicated rhythms.

When listening unconcernedly to the beats of the metronome when the interval between the beats is $\frac{1}{2}$ second or less, the above-described $\frac{4}{4}$ time generally appears. This groups together eight beats into one unity, whereas the $\frac{2}{8}$ time only embraces two beats. Now if we measure the scope of consciousness for such a complicated row of beats, we find that five bars of $\frac{4}{4}$ time can be grouped together and grasped as a whole; and if this row is repeated after a short interval, it can be recognised as identical with the preceding row. Here, then, we have forty beats as the scope of consciousness for this complicated rhythm, whereas with the most simple rhythmical arrangement we had only sixteen beats. This scope of forty seems to be the greatest we can attain by any means. We can, it is true, voluntarily call forth more complicated rhythmic arrangements, *e.g.* $\frac{6}{4}$ time. But such an increase in the number of beats in the rhythmic arrangement demands a certain exertion, and the length of the row that can be grouped together as one whole does not increase, but decreases.

In these experiments a further remarkable

quality of consciousness appears, which is closely connected to the rhythmical disposition of consciousness. The three degrees of emphasis, which the diagram of 4/4 time shows, form a maximum of differentiation which cannot be surpassed. Counting the unaccented beat as well, we arrive at a scale of intensity of four grades as the highest limit in the gradation of the intensity of impressions. This value clearly determines the rhythmical arrangement of the whole row, and with it the comprehension of this in consciousness, just as on the contrary the rhythm of the beats determines the number of gradations in intensity, which are necessary in the arrangement of the row of beats as supports for the comprehension by consciousness. Both factors therefore stand in close relationship to each other. The rhythmical disposition of consciousness demands certain limits for the number of grades of emphasis, and these on their part demand that specific rhythmical disposition which is peculiar to the human consciousness.

The more extensive the rows of beats become, which we join together in the experiments described, the more clearly does another important phenomenon of consciousness appear. If we pay attention to the relation between a beat, perceived in a certain given moment, and one that has immediately preceded it, and if we further compare this latter with a beat further back in the row that is being grouped together as a whole, differences of a certain kind between all these impressions appear. They are quite different from the variations in intensity and emphasis. To describe them we do best to make use of expressions, which were first of all formed in all languages to describe the perception of visual impressions, where the same differences also appear and are relatively independent of differences in the intensity of light. These expressions are "clearness" and "distinctness." Their meanings almost coincide, but still they differ inasmuch as they denote different sides of the faculty of perception. "Clearness" refers more to the special constitution of the impression itself; "distinctness" to the relation of the impression to other impressions from which it seems to stand out. Let us transfer these conceptions in a generalised sense to the content of consciousness. One row of beats clearly shows in each of its separate elements the most varying degrees of clearness and distinctness. They all in a regular manner bear upon the beat that is affecting consciousness at the moment. This beat is the one that is most clear and most distinct. The ones immediately preceding are most like this one, whereas those that lie further back lose more and more in clearness. If the beat furthest away lies so far back that the impression has absolutely disappeared, then we speak in a picturesque way of a sinking beneath the threshold of consciousness. For the opposite process we have at once the picture of a rising above the threshold. In a similar sense for that gradual approach to the threshold of consciousness, which we notice in our experiments in the beats that lie further back, we use the expression "a darkening," and for the reverse process "a brightening" of the content of consciousness. With the use of these expressions we can formulate in the following manner the condition necessary for the comprehension of a whole consisting of many parts, *e.g.* a row of beats: a comprehension as a whole is possible as long as no part sinks beneath the threshold of consciousness. For the most obvious differences in the clearness and distinctness of the content of consciousness, we generally use two other expressions, which, like our former ones of darkening and brightening, illustrate the meaning. We say that that element of consciousness, which is mostly clearly apprehended, lies in the fixation-point of consciousness, and that all the rest belongs to the field of consciousness. In our metronome experiments, therefore, the beat, that is at the moment affecting consciousness, lies in this subjective fixation-point, whereas the preceding beats, the further back they stretch, the more do they belong merely to this subjective field. This latter we may picture to ourselves as a region surrounding the fixation-point, which becomes gradually darker towards the periphery and at last is bounded by the threshold of consciousness.

In this last figure of speech we have already suggested that the so-called fixation-point of consciousness denotes in general only the ideal middle point of a central region, within which several impressions can be clearly and distinctly apprehended. So in one row of beats the beat heard at a certain moment would lie within the fixation-point; yet the immediately preceding beats are still clear and distinct enough, in order to be included within the same narrow region, which contrasts with the more extensive field by reason of its greater clearness. The psychological process agrees also in this respect with the expressions we have borrowed from the sense of sight, where we have a single point of the field of vision as fixation-point, around which a great number of impressions may be clearly perceived. Only because of this are we able to apprehend a larger image in a single moment, *e.g.* to read a word. For this central part of the field of our consciousness, which immediately surrounds the subjective fixation-point, the practical necessity of language has already coined a word, which has been accepted by psychology. We call that psychical process, which is operative in the clear perception of a narrow region of the content of consciousness, attention. When impressions, or any other content, at a certain moment are remarkable for their special clearness in comparison to the other elements in consciousness, we say that they lie within the focus of attention. Keeping to our former figure, we imagine this as the central region that surrounds the subjective fixation-point, and it is cut off by a more or less clearly defined boundary-line from the larger and darker field that surrounds it. And this immediately gives rise to a new experimental problem, which forms an important supplement to the above-described measurement of the whole scope of consciousness. The problem consists in answering the question that immediately arises, How big is this narrower scope of attention?

Rhythmical rows of beats, because of the arrangement of the successive impressions in them, were excellently suited to determine the total scope of consciousness. But because of this very same quality they can give us little help in solving our second problem. For it is obvious that just that connection between the focus of attention and the wider field of consciousness, that the rhythm of a row of beats causes—this connection makes a clear boundary between these two regions impossible. We notice clearly enough that along with the beat that is directly affecting consciousness a few of the preceding ones also fall within the focus of attention, but how many remains uncertain. The sense of sight obviously offers us more favourable conditions. We must, however, first of all note the fact that the physiological conditions of vision in themselves limit the apprehension of an extended object, not taking into account the psychological boundary of clear perception. The keenest differentiation of impressions is limited to the so-called region of clearest vision, which surrounds the fixation-point. The reader can test this for himself by fixating the middle letter *o* in the following diagram of letters from a distance of about 20–25 cm., while keeping one eye closed.

We can in this position, by directing our attention alone to the outlying parts of the field of vision, still recognise letters, which lie at the sides of our figure, as, for example, t h m

m v x w a s f

l g i c s f p d t

z r a e n p r h v z l

r f u c t h f b n d s

k h e p n o t v b s i

n z l u c r k m d g n

d i n i w g e t v r f

s a t f l b p n k

m d w c k t g

p a v e r

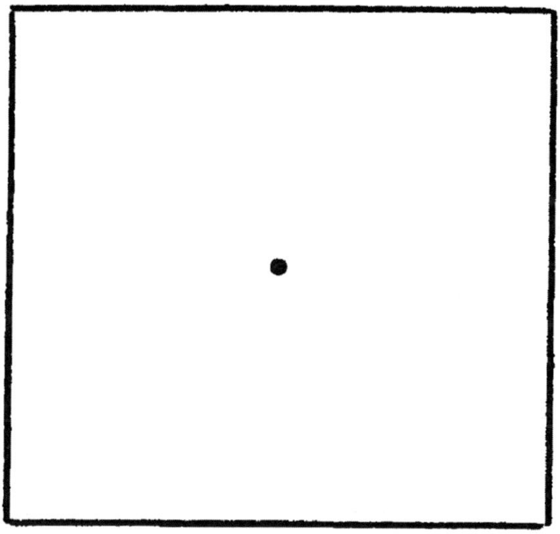

the *h* at the top or the *i* at the right-hand side. To carry out this experiment a little practice in fixation is required, since in natural vision we are always inclined to direct our line of vision to that point, to which our attention is turned. If, however, we practise letting our attention wander over the different parts of the field of vision while keeping the same fixation-point, it will soon be clear to us that the fixation-point of attention and the fixation-point of the field of vision are by no means identical. They can by practice be separated, and the attention can be directed to a point in indirect vision, *i.e.* a point lying to this or to that side of the line of vision. From this we see that clear perception in the psychological sense and clear vision in the physiological sense do not necessarily coincide. For example, if we fixate the middle letter *o*, and at the same time direct our attention to the *n* at the right-hand side, we also perceive clearly the letters that surround *n*, *i.e.* *f g s i*, whereas the letters around *o*, *i.e.* *h t ı n*, seem to retreat into the darker field of consciousness. This diagram of letters has been printed so large, that when we look at it from a distance of 20–25 cm. it almost corresponds in scope to the region of clearest vision, taking as a measure for this the recognisability of letters of the size of those printed in this book. We see, therefore, at once from the above-described observations, that the scope of the focus of attention and the region of clearest vision in the physiological sense differ widely from each other. The latter, under the conditions of observation we have chosen, comprises a far wider field than the former. In our figure there are 95 letters. If it were possible simultaneously clearly to perceive in the psychological sense all the objects clearly seen physiologically, then we should be able by fixating the point *o* to perceive all these letters. This is, however, by no means the case. At one given moment we can differentiate only a few, which surround the fixation-point of attention, whether this coincides with the objective fixation-point of the field of vision, as in ordinary vision, or whether it lies in any way outside of this point owing to a severance of the two fixation-points.

Although these observations as to the simultaneous recognition of haphazardly arranged simple objects, *e.g.* letters, point decisively to a fairly narrow limitation of the scope of attention, still we cannot give an exact numerical answer by this method as to the size of this scope, as we could by means of our metronome experiments in regard to the scope of consciousness. Still, without any great change and without any complicated apparatus, we can make these visual experiments suffice to answer our question. Our immediate results will, of course, only be valid under the special conditions we set up. For this purpose a great number of such diagrams, with letters arranged in the same manner, must be constructed. The position of the letters in each diagram must be different. Then a fairly large square of white cardboard, with a black point in the middle, is made (as in the figure on p. 19). With this we cover the diagram chosen for the experiment. The observer, who previously must not have seen the diagrams, is told to fixate with one eye the point in the middle, and to keep the other eye closed.

The cover is then taken away rapidly for one moment, and then as rapidly replaced. The rapidity of this procedure must be such that no movement of the eye, or wandering of the attention over the field of vision, can take place, as long as the diagram remains uncovered.[1] Each time we repeat the experiment a new diagram must be chosen, otherwise the individual momentary impression will supplement the preceding ones. If we wish to obtain unambiguous results we must choose conditions which exclude such influences of previous perceptions. Our question will therefore be limited to this: What is the number of simple and new impressions in consciousness that the focus of attention can grasp in one given moment? In reference to this way of stating the question, an objection to our method of experimenting might be raised. It might be objected that a letter is not a

[1] To carry out such experiments more exactly and more uniformly it is best to make use of the simple apparatus called the tachistoscope. A falling screen exposes the object to sight for a very short time, which can be accurately measured. Still, if this apparatus cannot be procured, the procedure described above suffices. Special practice should be devoted to covering and uncovering the diagram, so that this may be done as rapidly as possible.

simple element of consciousness, and that we ought rather to use simpler objects, *e.g.* dots. But since these lack all means of differentiation, the carrying out of the experiment would be rendered much more difficult, if not impossible. On the other hand, we must not forget that our familiarity with letters is of the greatest importance. Because of this a letter of ordinary print can be perceived as quickly as a single dot—a fact any one can easily prove for himself by means of observation. Such symbols, because of their characistic differences, have this advantage, that after a momentary impression they can be easily retained in consciousness, and thus an account of what has been clearly perceived can be given after the experiment. If we carry out the experiments in the manner described, it appears that an unpractised observer can perceive, at most, only 3–4 letters. After a few more experiments this number increases to 6. Of course, as before mentioned, a new diagram must be used in every new experiment. This value 6 cannot be increased by further practice, and it remains the same for different observers. We are therefore entitled to regard it as a constant for attention for the human consciousness.

This determination of the scope of attention is, however, dependent upon one condition, which is exactly the opposite of that introduced in measuring the scope of consciousness. This latter was only possible by using rows of impressions that were bound together into one complex whole. To measure the scope of attention, on the other hand, we must isolate the separate impressions from each other, so that they form an unarranged multiplicity of elements. This is a difference in conditions which certainly does not only depend upon the fact that in the first case the sense of hearing and in the second case the sense of sight was used. We rather conjecture at the very outset that here the chief influence lay in the psychological conditions, in the first case in the combination of the elements into a whole, and in the second in the isolation of the elements. At once the following question naturally arises: What will happen if we, so to speak, change the rôles of these two senses, if we let impressions, connected together as wholes, work upon the sense of sight, and isolated impressions upon the sense of hearing? In the first case we have simply to combine letters together, so that they form words or sentences. A letter is nothing more than an element that has been artificially taken out of such a natural combination. Now if we carry out with these parts of speech experiments in the same manner as we have described above, we obtain, in fact, an absolutely different result. If we show the observer a word such as this—

Miscellaneousness,

he can read it at once, without being prepared for it and without previous practice. With isolated elements he could at most grasp six, but here, under exactly the same conditions, the scope is extended to seventeen or more elements without the slightest difficulty. It is clear that this is essentially the same phenomenon that we encountered in our experiments on rhythm with the sense of hearing. The conditions of combination are, however, in so far different, as the stimuli for the sense of sight were simultaneous, whereas for the sense of hearing the whole was made up of simple impressions that followed each other. And with this another difference is connected. A word can only be recognised at a momentary glance, if it has been known to us before as a whole, or with compound words, if their chief parts have been familiar to us. Therefore a word of an absolutely unknown language appears as a complex of unarranged letters, and with such a complex our scope is again limited to six isolated elements. With a rhythmical row of beats, on the other hand, it is of no consequence what the form of rhythm is that binds them together, since we can think into such a row whatever rhythmical arrangement we choose, as long as it conforms to the general rhythmical disposition of consciousness, *i.e.* as long as it does not exceed the maximum of three different accents, as we have previously shown. At the same time this requirement shows us that the differences in apprehending a successive and a simultaneous whole, which appear in our experiments with sight and hearing, are in reality only apparent differences. A musical time that is adequate to our sense of rhythm behaves in exactly the same way as a word or sentence that is adequate to our sense of language. Therefore we may presuppose that in the reading, as in the rhythm experiments, it is not the whole of a complex consisting of many elements that is instantaneously grasped by the attention. Only a limited part of such a word falls within the scope of attention, and from this part the psychical power of combination goes over to those other elements that lie in the wider field of consciousness. In fact there is a well-known phenomenon that gives a striking proof for this combination of the parts of a word or sentence grasped by attention with unclearly perceived elements. It consists in the fact that misprints are so often unnoticed, especially in rapid reading. This would be impossible if we were forced to perceive with our attention equally clearly all the separate elements of a long word or of a sentence in order to be able to read. In fact, in each separate moment there are only a few elements within the focus of attention. From these the threads of psychical combination stretch to the elements unclearly perceived—

yes, sometimes even to the impressions only physiologically seen that lie in the regions of indirect vision. Just as in hearing a rhythm, the sound impressions affecting consciousness at the moment are bound to the preceding ones that have retreated into the darker regions of consciousness, and, on the other hand, they are preparing the way for further expected impressions. The chief difference of the two cases lies not so much in the formal relations of the scope of attention and of consciousness, as in the constitution of the elements and their combinations.

Let us now, equipped with the results of our visual experiments, turn our attention again to our metronome experiments. The analogy between the two immediately gives rise to this question: Can we not in our rhythm experiments arrange the conditions so that we may obtain a similar isolation of simple impressions, as was necessary in measuring the scope of attention for the sense of sight? Now in fact such an isolation of single beats arises at once, as soon as we restrain a "hearing into" the beats of any kind of accentuation whatever. Even the simplest rhythm, the $\frac{2}{8}$ time, must be avoided. This is not so easy as it appears to be at the first glance, because of the rhythmical disposition of our consciousness and of our whole psycho-physical organisation. Again and again we are inclined to hear into a row of beats following each other at similar intervals, at least the $\frac{2}{8}$ time. And yet it is possible to conform to this condition, if the metronome beats do not show any noticeable objective differences. The interval between the beats must be chosen long enough to check any tendency to rhythmical grouping, and yet not too long, so that it may still remain possible to grasp so many beats as one whole. In general an interval of from $1\frac{1}{2}$–$2\frac{1}{2}$ seconds will conform to this requirement. With such an interval, after a fair amount of practice, it is possible to change at will from a rhythmical to an unrhythmical or absolutely monotonous perception of the beats. If this is done, and if in exactly the same manner as in the rhythm experiments a number of metronome beats is given, and then after a pause the same or a slightly differing number is given, the observer can clearly perceive the identity or difference of the two rows. If in the first test a row of six beats is given (row A), and in the second a row of nine, it appears in repeating two rows of the same length, that a precise recognition of identity is present with row A, whereas with row B this is impossible. Even with seven or eight beats recognition is very uncertain. We arrive

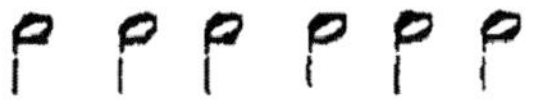

Row A.

Row B.

therefore at the same result as in our optical experiments. Six simple impressions form the limit for the scope of attention.

Since this value is the same for optical and acoustical, for successive and simultaneous impressions, it surely denotes some psychical constant independent of any special sense. And in fact in using different kinds of impressions we always arrive at the same result. The number six with very minor variations denotes the maximum of simple impressions that can be grasped by attention. If we choose syllables of any form, that are not combined into words, and if we read out a row of such to an observer, and require him to repeat them, we find that a correct repetition is possible with a row such as the following:—

ap ku no li sa ro

Whereas it is not possible with a row like this:—

ra po su am na il ok pu

We notice that even with seven such senseless syllables the repetition is generally unsuccessful. We may by practice become successful with seven syllables. This is obviously exactly the same result as we obtained above with our rows of metronome beats.

There still remains another phenomenon that coincides with this result. It is the more worthy of note since it belongs to a third sense, namely the sense of touch, and since it was discovered from practical considerations quite independent of psychology. There had been many futile attempts to discover the most useful method of printing for the blind, before Braille, a French teacher of the blind, about the middle of last century solved this important practical problem. He himself had become blind, and was therefore in a better position than others to make sure of the requirements that were necessary, by means of experiments upon himself. He came to this result, that, first of all, groups of distinct points were the only suitable means of establishing letter-signs that could be easily distinguished, and that, secondly, not more than six definite points were to be used for one letter. These points must not spread over an extent greater than that which can be covered by the sense of touch, if the symbols are to be distinguished by the fingers of the blind with ease and certainty. He decided for an arrangement of points as seen in Fig. I., out of which the alphabet for the blind was arranged :—

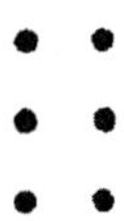

FIG. I.

a g e q o

FIG. II.

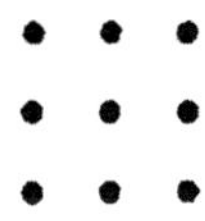

FIG. III.

This limitation to six points in certain positions certainly did not come about by chance.

This can clearly be seen from the fact that a greater number, *e.g.* an arrangement of nine points as in Fig. III., would have greater practical advantages. By means of them it would have been possible for example to represent the most important punctuation marks or numbers with separate signs, a thing which is not possible in Braille's type for the blind. But such complications in the positions of the points are at once made useless by the fact that it is impossible clearly to grasp the difference of such a large number of points. Any one can convince himself of this by immediate observation, if he arranges more than six similar signs and tries to distinguish by touch alone. Thus we arrive again at the same limit that our metronome and optical experiments led us to.

The importance of these results as to the scope of consciousness and of attention does not lie merely in the fact that we are able to state the relation of both in values that can be expressed in figures. Above all, our results give us an important insight into the relations between those elements that stand in the focus of attention and those that belong to the wider field of consciousness. In order, then, to denote clearly the most important results that have come to light in these experiments, let us use two short expressions for the two processes of the entrance into consciousness, and of the elevation into the focus of attention—two expressions that were first of all introduced by Leibnitz in a similar sense. We shall call the entrance into the large region of consciousness—apprehension, and the elevation into the focus of attention —apperception. We shall take no account of the philosophical meanings, in which Leibnitz uses these expressions in his theory of monads. We shall use these expressions purely in their empirical and psychological sense. Accordingly we understand by apprehension simply the entrance of some content into consciousness—an entrance that can be in fact proved, and by apperception the grasping of this by the attention. The apprehended content is that of which we are more or less darkly aware; it is always, however, above the threshold of consciousness. The apperceived content is that of which we are clearly aware, or, keeping to the figure of speech of a threshold, that which lies above the narrower threshold of attention. We can further define the relation between these two regions of consciousness. If the apperception is directed to one isolated element, the rest, the merely psychically apprehended elements, disappear as if they were non-existent. On the other hand, if the apperceived content is bound to certain merely apprehended elements of consciousness, it is combined into one total apprehension, which is only limited by the threshold of consciousness itself. In close relationship with this stands the fact that the scope of apperception is a relatively limited and constant one, and that the scope of apprehension is not only larger, but also much more variable. And, as we have clearly seen from our comparison of simple and complex rhythmical rows, it varies according to the scope of the psychical complexes that are united together into one whole. Thereby the difference between the merely apprehended and the apperceived parts of such a whole by no means disappears. For it is only a limited part of this latter that lies within the focus of attention, as has been strikingly shown in reading experiments, where we can vary single and merely apprehended parts of a word, without thereby disturbing the comprehension of the total complex. To use a picture which is itself an example of this phenomenon, we may say that that wider darkly apprehended content stands in the same relation here as the chords of the piano accompaniment to the voice of the singer. Slight variations in the former are mostly unobserved, so long as the guiding voice is correct in pitch and rhythm. On the other hand, the impression of the whole would be feeble if the accompaniment was wanting.

In this relationship between the apprehended and apperceived content of consciousness another factor appears, which brings to light the great importance of the processes of apperception. We started out from the fact that it was extremely difficult to apprehend with absolute uniformity a row of identical beats, since we are always inclined to accentuate certain beats. This phenomenon is clearly connected with a fundamental characteristic of apperception, which intervenes in all processes of consciousness. We know, from ordinary life, that we are not able to direct our attention perfectly steadily and uniformly to one and the same object. When we attempt to do this, we notice that a continual change takes place in the apperception of the object in question. At times the attention turns towards the object most intensively, and at times its energy flags. Where the conditions remain uniform, this change gradually becomes regular and periodic. The rise of such a process is of course materially assisted, if the outside impressions themselves, to which our attention is directed, possess a regular periodicity. This is the case in a high degree with a row of beats. And so it happens that those oscillations of apperception are directly adjusted to the periodicity of the impressions. Therefore we emphasise an impression that coincides with a rise in the apperception wave, so that the beats which are in fact uniform become rhythmically arranged. The manner of this arrangement depends to a certain degree upon our own choice, and also upon the extent in which we are trying to combine the single impressions into a whole. If the beats follow each other very quickly, our endeavour to combine leads us easily into complicated rhythmical arrangements, as we have in fact noticed above. With other and especially with simultaneous impressions similar relations between the apperceived and the merely apprehended content of consciousness arise, but in varying form according to the sense in question. For example, if we expose a very short word in our reading experiments, the whole is easily apprehended at one glance. If, however, we expose a long word, *e.g.* "miscellaneousness," we notice at once, even by direct observation, that the apprehension time is a little longer and that it really is made up of two or three very rapid and successive acts of apperception, and these acts may last longer than the actual time the impression is affecting consciousness. This succession is seen more clearly, if instead of a word we expose a sentence of about the same length as the following:—

"Honesty is the best policy."

Here the breaking up of apperception into successive acts is materially assisted by the divisions of the words. With such a sentence we observe as a rule three successive acts of apperception, and it is the last that combines the whole into one unified thought. In such a case this is only possible as long as the preceding parts of the sentence from the last apperception remain in the field of consciousness. If the sentence is so long that this cannot happen, then the same thing occurs as we have observed with rhythmical rows of beats, that have passed the limits of possible rhythmical arrangement. We can only combine a part of such a successively exposed whole into one conclusive act of apperception. It is obvious therefore that the two phenomena, the apprehension of connected beats and of connected words and sentences, are essentially the same. The only difference consists in the fact that in the first case the apperceived impression is connected with the preceding one, that has retreated into the apprehension field, by means of the rhythmical arrangement, whereas the connection in the second case is brought about by means of the sense that binds the word or the parts of the word together. The process consists by no means of a mere successive apperception of the parts. These have already disappeared out of the apperception and have become merely apprehended elements, when they are combined into one whole along with the last apperceived impression. This act of combination is itself a uniform and instantaneous act of apperception. From this we see that, in all cases of a combination of a larger complex of elements, apperception is the function that unites these elements, and that in general it always combines directly apperceived parts of the whole with the merely apprehended parts that stand in connection. And so the great importance of the relations between these two functions of apperception and of apprehension lies precisely in the great change of these relations and in their adjustment to the needs of our psychical life, which finds expression in this change of relation to each other. At times the apperception concentrates upon a very narrow region, in order completely to free itself from the enormous manifoldness of incoming impressions. At other times, with the help of its capacity for grouping together successive elements which arises from the oscillating nature of its function, it winds its threads through a wide web of psychical contents, that stretches over the whole field of consciousness. Through it all apperception remains the unifying function which binds that manifold content into one ordered whole. Contrasted with it and subordinate to it, and in a certain sense acting as centrifugal forces, are the processes of apprehension, which with apperception together form the whole of our psychical life.

## CHAPTER II

### THE ELEMENTS OF CONSCIOUSNESS

In our last chapter we have discussed the general and formal characteristics of consciousness. These have appeared to us in the scope of consciousness, in the different grades of clearness and distinctness of its content, and lastly, connected with this, in the relations of apprehension and apperception. The next question that immediately presents itself is: Of what kind is the specific content that appears to us in these forms? The answer to this question includes the task of explaining the ultimate parts of this content, that cannot be further disintegrated. Such ultimate parts are generally called elements. Now it is one of the first tasks of each science, that deals with the investigation of empirical facts, to discover the elements of the phenomena. Its second task is to find out the laws according to which these elements enter into combinations. The whole task of psychology can therefore be summed up in these two problems: (1) What are the elements of consciousness? (2) What combinations do these elements undergo and what laws govern these combinations?

In contradistinction to the elements of consciousness let us call any combination of such elements a psychical compound. The relation of the two to each other can be at once made clear by the examples that lie at hand. Let us return to our metronome. If we let one single beat work upon consciousness and then immediately arrest the pendulum, we have a psychical element. Such a beat cannot in general be further disintegrated if we, as can easily be done in such a case, abstract from the fact that we hear it from some special direction in space, &c. If, on the other hand, we let two beats work, they constitute at once a psychical compound. This becomes always more complex, the more such beats we combine into a row, and the more we increase this complication by different degrees of accentuation, as in the examples of $\frac{2}{8}$ and $\frac{4}{4}$ time described above. Such an element of consciousness as the single beat is called a sensation, a combination of elements into rhythms of more or less complicated constitution is called an idea. Even at the present time many psychologists use the word "idea" only for a complex that does not arise from direct outward impressions, *i.e.* only for so-called "memory images." For ideas formed by outward sense impressions they generally use the word "perception." Now this distinction is psychologically of absolutely no importance, since there are really no valid differences between memory ideas and so-called sense-perceptions. The memory ideas of our dreams are in general quite as lively as sense impressions in the waking state, and it is for this reason that they are often held to be really experienced phenomena. The word "idea" denotes well the essential characteristic of all these complexes. The idea (Greek ἰδέα) is the form or appearance of something in the outer world. In the same sense, as belonging to the outer world, we speak of the sensations and their complexes arising in our own body as organic sensations, because we locate them in our own body, *e.g.* the sensations of fatigue of our muscles, the pressure and pain sensations of the inner organs, &c. The relatively uniform elements of touch and organic sensations are distributed among the sensations of pressure, warmth, cold, and pain. In contradistinction to these, the special senses of hearing, seeing, smelling, and tasting present an abundance of sensations, each of which, according to its peculiar constitution, is called a quality of sensation. Each such quality is oesides variable in its intensity. We can, for example, produce a certain beat in very wariable intensities, while the quality remains the same.

In all these cases we meet with the same relations between sensations and ideas, as we saw in the metronome beats described above. Green or red, white or black, &c., are called wisual sensations; a green surface or a black body is called a visual idea. The relation is exactly the same as between the single beat and the row of beats. Only in this case the combination of several sensations to an idea of a surface or of a body forces itself upon us much more directly, and it requires a very careful abstraction from this combination into an ideational complex, in order to retain the conception of a sensation. But we can vary our ideas of surfaces and bodies at will, while the colour remains the same. So at last we are forced to look upon this element, that remains the same in spite of all changes in the combinations, as a simple sensation. In the same way we consider a simple tone as a sensation of hearing, and a clang or chord, composed of several tones, as an auditory idea, and so on. If the tones follow each other in a melodious and rhythmical combination, then ideas of increasing complexity arise, and in the same manner several relatively simple visual ideas may be bound together into more extensive simultaneous or successive unities. The senses of sight and of hearing in especial form in this way a great variety of sensations and ideas, and they do this in two ways—firstly, through the qualities of their simple sensations, and secondly, through the complications of ideas, into which these sensations may be combined. The simple scale of tones, from the deepest to the highest tone that can be heard, consists of an infinite gradation of tonal qualities, out of which our musical scale chooses only certain tones, which lie at relatively large distances from each other. Musical clangs are combinations of a number of such simple tonal sensations, and the so-called compound clangs increase this complicated constitution of the clangs by emphasising to a greater degree certain partial tones. The simple light-sensations form a more concise manifoldness, but one that stretches into different directions. Red, for example, on the one hand goes over by constant gradations into orange and then into yellow, and on the other hand we have just as many constant gradations from each of these colour-shades through the lighter colour-tones into white, or through the darker ones into black, and so on. The ideas of this sense are absolutely inexhaustible. If we think of the manifold forms of surfaces and bodies, and of the differences in distance and direction, in which we perceive objects, it is obvious that it is absolutely impossible to find any limit here. Thus the richness in sensations and ideas, which each of the senses conveys, stands in close relation to the spatial distance of the objects which they introduce into consciousness. The narrowest region is that of the touch and organic sense, where the impressions all refer to our own body. Then come the sensations of the two so-called chemical senses of taste and of smell. Even in man they have the important function of organs of help or protection in the choice of food, as is the case in the whole animal kingdom. The sensations and ideas of hearing stretch much further. By means of them the outer world enters into relation with our consciousness in language, song, and music. And last of all, the sense of sight, the sense of distance in the real meaning of the word, gives form and content to the whole picture of the outer world, that we carry in our consciousness.

However different the qualities of sensations and the forms of ideas may be, yet these elements and complexes all agree in one particular—they all refer to the objective world, to things and processes outside of us, to their qualities, their combinations, and their relations. Our own body, to which touch and organic sensations relate, forms in contradistinction to our consciousness a part of this outer world. It is the nearest to us, but still a mere part of the outer world. The question immediately arises: Do these objective elements and complexes form the only content of consciousness? Or in other words, are the only psychical elements such as we project outwards? Or are there in our consciousness, besides this picture of the outer world, other elements, which we do not apprehend as objects or their qualities that stand in contradistinction to ourselves?

To answer this question let us use the metronome to help us. If we choose time intervals of a medium length, say ½ to 1½ seconds, and if we make such a row of beats rhythmical by the voluntary emphasis of certain beats in the manner described above, then each single beat represents a sensation and the whole row of beats represents an idea. At the same time, during the impression on consciousness of such a rhythmical whole we notice phenomena that are not contained in our definition of sensation or idea. Above all, we have at the end of the row of beats the impression of an agreeable whole. If we wish to define this concept of "agreeable" more accurately, we may describe it as a subjective feeling of pleasure, which is caused by outward impressions, which we therefore call agreeable. This concept consists therefore of two parts—an objective idea, in our case the row of beats, and a subjective feeling of pleasure. This latter is obviously not in itself included in the impression of the row of beats or in that which we call the idea. It is clearly an added subjective element. It also shows itself to be such from the fact that we do not project it into the outer world. It is apprehended directly as a reaction of our consciousness, or rather, to express it at once more fittingly, of our apperception. This shows itself also in the relative independence of this feeling of pleasure from the objective constitution of the impression. Since in such a simple compound as a rhythmical row of beats the agreeableness is generally very moderate, we clearly observe that with many individuals the feeling of pleasure contained in it often sinks below the threshold of consciousness, so that they only perceive the objective constitution of the beats. With others this subjective reaction becomes very prominent. The feeling of pleasure will, as is well known, become more intense, when harmonious tones combine with the rhythmical beat into one melodious whole. The agreeable feeling that then arises from the melody can scarcely be wanting in any individual consciousness. Just here we note that the degree of this feeling of pleasure for one and the same melody can vary extraordinarily for different individuals. And these subjective differences increase more and more as the melodious compound becomes more complicated. A complicated tone-structure may produce the greatest ecstasy in a musician, whereas it may leave an unmusical person absolutely cold. The latter, on the other hand, may perhaps find a very simple melody agreeable, and this same melody may appear trivial to the musician and therefore disagreeable. In all these cases we see that the feeling of pleasure, which is bound to certain sensations and ideas, is purely subjective. It is an element that is not only dependent upon the impression itself, but also and always and most of all dependent upon the subject receiving the impression. And negatively the subjective character of this feeling is shown in the fact that it is never projected into the outer world, although it may be so closely bound up with the idea that refers to the outer world.

But feelings of pleasure are not the only ones that we observe in our rhythm experiments. If we call to mind the exact state of consciousness between two beats of a rhythmical row, we notice that the apprehension of the identity of two intervals arises by means of a subjective process. This process takes place in the same manner within each of the two compared intervals, and thereby gives rise to the impression that they coincide. In ordinary life we generally speak of the phenomena, that are observed in such cases, as a change from "expectation" to "realisation." If we follow these phenomena a little more closely, we notice that in our case the process of expectation is a continuous and regularly varying one. At the moment immediately following one beat, expectation strains itself to catch the next one, and this straining increases until this beat really occurs. At the same moment the strain is suddenly relieved by the realisation of the expected, when the new beat comes. Then the same process is repeated during the next interval. If the arrangement of the beat is more complicated because of different degrees of emphasis, then these subjective processes become in proportion more complicated, since several such processes of expectation and realisation overlap one another.

What do these processes, which we so often meet, although not always in such regular change as in a rhythmical row of beats, consist of? It is obvious at a glance that expectation and realisation are both elements that are not bound to the objective impression itself. These processes can vary subjectively just as much as the agreeable feeling that arises from a rhythmical row of beats or from a melody. It is now pretty generally agreed that these peculiar elements of consciousness arise within us and not without us. There is, however, still one possibility that remains. It might be that sensations are the bearers of these subjective phenomena of expectation, perhaps sensations that are perceived while listening to a row of beats, arising partly in the interior of the ear because of the straining of the membrane of the tympanum, and partly in the mimic muscles that surround the ear. These sensations correspond to the similar sensations in the eye in expectation of visual impressions. Yet this hypothesis, on closer examination, proves untenable for various reasons. First of all these sensations continue, during the whole period of expectation, in a relatively constant intensity, as far as can be observed. There is no trace of that regular increase and that sudden transition to the opposite process of realisation, such as we observed in our rhythm experiments. Secondly, we can produce exactly similar sensations in our ear, or round about our ear, or in the region surrounding the eye, if we voluntarily contract the muscles in question, without our being in a state of expectation, or if we send a slight electric current through such muscles. In both cases the characteristic element of expectation is wanting. Lastly, it is obviously impossible to account for these phenomena by means of uniform muscle-sensations if we wish to explain that superposition of states of expectation of different degrees and extents, which we observed in more complicated rhythmical rows of beats, or which happens in complicated psychical states arising through intellectual processes. How could the sensations of the membrane of the tympanum, or of the fixation muscles of the eye, account for that intense feeling of expectation which an exciting novel or a good play may cause? Add to this the fact that these states are quite as subjective and dependent on the individual disposition of consciousness as a feeling of pleasure that is awakened by an agreeable rhythm, and it is at once obvious that these states, which we shall call for shortness the contrasts of strain and relaxation, have the very same right to be called feelings. For feelings, wherever they arise, accompany, as subjective reactions of consciousness, sensations and ideas, but are never identical with them.

We obtain therefore, with the above-mentioned medium rapidity of the metronome, feelings of pleasure and feelings of strain and relaxation in close connection with each other, as regular concomitants of rhythmical impressions. This, however, is essentially changed if the rapidity of the beats is altered. If we chose intervals of from 2½ to 3 seconds, strain and relaxation follow similarly as before. They appear even more distinctly, since the strain increases to a greater intensity because of the longer intervals. But just as distinctly does the feeling of pleasure decrease with this increase in the length of the interval, and we soon reach the limit where the strain of expectation becomes painful. Here, then, the former feeling of pleasure is transformed into a feeling of displeasure, which is again closely connected with the feelings of strain and relaxation. Now let us proceed in the opposite direction by making the metronome beats follow each other after intervals of ½ to ¼ of a second, and we notice that the feelings of strain and relaxation disappear. In their place appears an excitement that increases with the rapidity of the impressions, and along with this we have generally a more or less lively feeling of displeasure. We see, therefore, a new feeling added to those already found. We may call it most appropriately excitation. It is sufficiently well known to us in ordinary life in its more complicated forms, where it obviously forms an essential component of many emotions, *e.g.* anger, lively joy, &c. We can also find the contrast to this feeling of excitation with the help of the same instrument, by suddenly decreasing the rapidity of the beats to their medium rapidity again. This change is regularly accompanied by a very distinct feeling of quiescence (a quieting or subduing feeling).

Accordingly our metronome experiments have brought to light three pairs of feelings —pleasure and pain, strain and relaxation, excitation and quiescence. At the same time it has been shown that only very seldom do these forms of feeling appear isolated. Several of them are generally combined together into one feeling-compound. We may call this latter the aggregate feeling, and the former the partial feelings. It is evident that between these two a similar relation exists as between ideas and pure sensations. Besides this, the contrasts of each pair of feelings —*e.g.* pleasure and displeasure—include the possibility of all these contrasts balancing each other, so that a state almost free from feeling may result. Just as, on the other hand, several partial feelings very often join together to form one aggregate feeling, so in more complicated states of emotion contrasting feelings may be intertwined. They do not therefore in all cases compensate one another. They sometimes join together to make contrasting combinations. Simple cases of such contrasting combinations or disjointed moods can be brought about in a simple form by means of the metronome. We arrange the time of the beats so that the feeling of strain just begins to become painful, while at the same time the feeling of relaxation, and partly also the strain directed on this, still causes pleasure.

Let us now leave rhythmical acoustical impressions and consider any other sense. We find everywhere the same pairs of feelings that we produced by means of the metronome. It is very striking how the feeling-character always follows in the same directions, if we give successive impressions that give rise to contrasting feelings. Red is exciting, while blue in contrast to it is quieting. In the same way a deep and a high tone contrast. At the same time, the feeling-contrast is here a mixed one, as the expressions "serious" and "solemn" for deep tones, and "bright" and "lively" for the high ones, show. It would seem as if with the deepest tones pleasure and displeasure combine together to that total impression of seriousness, and to this a quieting feeling is added when the deep tone stands in contrast to preceding high tones.

The feelings joined to the impressions of the senses of touch and smell and taste are in general more uniform and simpler. Here we have as contrasts the strong displeasure of a sensation of pain, and the feeling of pleasure of a weak sensation of tickling. Similarly with the pleasant impression of a sweet and the unpleasant impression of an intensely bitter or sour taste, and so on. It is obvious, however, that already among the smells we find many that possess a composite feeling-quality, *e.g.* pleasant and at the same time exciting, as menthol-ether, or unpleasant and exciting, as ammonia and asafœtida. The organic or common sensations are also often of a mixed feeling-character. Yet pleasure and displeasure predominate here most of all.

An important characteristic of feelings consists lastly in the fact that they combine themselves into an affective process, which as a rule is joined to an ideational process. A temporal process of this kind with an affective and ideational content, that changes but is nevertheless joined together, we call an emotion, or with less intensity and a more lasting nature of the feelings, a disposition. Joy, delight, merriness, hope are emotions in which the predominant feeling is pleasure; anger, grief, sorrow, and fear are emotions in which displeasure predominates. Now in both these series of emotions the exciting and quieting feelings and the feelings of strain and relaxation in many cases often play an important part. The quieting feeling combined with displeasure we call depression. Joy and anger are exciting emotions, grief and fear are depressing, hope, sorrow, and fear are straining. When, however, an expected result takes place, or when the emotion of fear disappears, a strong feeling of relaxation generally occurs. Many emotions are also characterised by a fluctuating affective process, sometimes changing in intensity and sometimes in quality. Anger, hope, and sorrow in especial show great fluctuations in intensity. With hope, fear, and sorrow we very often find fluctuations in quality. Hope and sorrow often change between themselves, and in most cases increase in intensity because of this contrast. Especially with the emotions we can perceive this affective process objectively in the movements of the mimic muscles of the face, and when the emotions are very strong in the other muscles of the body. These so-called mimic and pantomimic "expression movements" are always combined with characteristic changes of the movements of the heart and lungs. They are in so far the most sensitive characteristics of these subjective processes, since they can be observed even with the weakest emotions and even with the simplest feelings, that have not yet been bound together into an affective process. The expansion and contraction of the small blood-vessels, especially of the face, that often happens in a state of emotion, must also be mentioned here. In anger and shame we notice blushing, and in fear and fright pallor.

A further class of important compound processes stands in close connection with the emotions, *i.e.* the volitional processes. In many cases, even at the present day, the will is held to be a specific psychical element, or it is considered in its essence to be identical with the idea of an intended act. A closer investigation of the volitional process as to its subjective and objective characteristics shows, however, that it is most closely connected with the emotions, and that it really is to be considered an affective process. There is no act of volition in which feelings of greater or less intensity, which combine into an affective process, are not present. The characteristic in which a volitional process differs from an emotion consists essentially in the end of the process that immediately precedes and accompanies the act of volition. If this end is not reached, it remains simply an emotion. We speak of the emotion of anger if a man merely shows his angry excitement in his expression movements. On the other hand we speak of an act of emotion if he fells to the ground the person who has excited his anger. In many cases the emotions and their feeling-content, which form the constituent parts of the volitional process, are weaker, but they are never absolutely wanting. A voluntary action without feeling, one that follows from purely intellectual motives, as many philosophers presuppose, does not exist at all. On the other hand the volitional processes are marked out from the ordinary emotions by characteristics which give volition its peculiar character. Firstly there are certain ideas in the process which possess a more or less strong feeling-tone, and which are in direct connection with the end stage of the act of volition, and prepare for it. We call such ideas the motives of volition. Secondly, the end stage consists of characteristic feelings, which always occur in essentially the same manner in all volitional processes. These we generally call feelings of activity. They are very probably compounded of feelings of excitation, of strain, and of relaxation, as a closer subjective analysis and the concomitant objective expression-symptoms, especially the movements of breathing, show. Excitation and strain precede the conclusive act, relaxation and excitation accompany the act, and continue for a short time afterwards. It is obvious that the number and the reciprocal action of the motives are of decisive moment for the constitution of the volitional process. If only one single motive is present, which prepares the emotion and its discharge into action, we call the volitional process an impulsive act. The acts of animals are clearly in most cases such simple volitional acts. So also in the psychical life of man they play a very important part—the leading part in the more composite volitional processes, and they very often arise out of these latter when these have been often repeated. The actions that arise out of several conflicting motives of strong feeling-tone we call voluntary acts, or if we are clearly aware of a previous conflict of opposite motives, selective or discriminative acts. According to this complication of motives, the end stage, which is especially characteristic of the volitional processes, takes different forms. With impulsive acts the whole process takes place quickly; the concluding feelings of excitation, strain, and relaxation are generally crowded together in a very short time. With voluntary and especially with selective acts, the whole process is much slower, and the feelings often fluctuate up and down. The same is often the case with those complex volitional acts, which do not show themselves outwardly in certain bodily movements, but which give rise to changes in the process of consciousness itself. Such inner volitional acts are noticed above all in the voluntary concentration of attention, in the direction of thought guided by special motives, and so on.

Now if we investigate more closely these feelings of strain, excitation, and relaxation, which make up these inner volitional acts, we notice at once the great conformity of these with the processes which accompany the apperception of an impression or of an idea arising in consciousness through recollection. It is obvious that these elements, grouped together under the name of "feelings of activity," make up along with varying sensations the essential part of impulsive and voluntary acts in the one case, and of the processes of attention and apperception in the other. These processes also coincide in so far as different forms of apperception correspond to impulsive and voluntary action. If we apprehend an impression which is given to us without our assistance, the attention seems in a sense to be compelled to turn to this impression, following this single motive. We can express this by saying we apprehend it passively. The feeling of activity always follows such an impression. If on the other hand we turn to an expected impression, then these feelings of strain and excitation clearly precede the impression. We are aware that our apperception is active. These have often been called processes of involuntary and voluntary attention. But these expressions are unsuitable, since in reality volitional processes are present in both cases. They are, like impulsive and voluntary acts, merely processes of different grades. It is at once evident that, by reason of this inner conformity, apperception itself may be looked upon as a volitional process. It occurs as an essential factor in all inner and outer volitional acts, and as an ever-present one in the feelings of activity so characteristic of the will. Herein lies the chief motive for the fact that we look upon the will as our most private possession, the one that is most identical with our inner nature itself. Our ideas seem in comparison with it to be something external, upon which our will reacts according to its feelings. And so at bottom our will coincides with our "ego." Now this ego is neither an idea, nor a specific feeling, but it consists of those elementary volitional processes of apperception which accompany the processes of consciousness. They are always changing but they are always present, and in this way form the lasting substratum of our self-consciousness. The inner line of fortifications of this ego are the feelings, which represent nothing more than the reactions of apperception to outer experience. The next line consists of this experience itself—the ideas, of which the ones that are nearest to us, *i.e.* those of our own body, are most closely connected with the volitional processes that are at work in the apprehension of them. And so it happens at a naïve stage of consciousness that they are combined together with the ego itself into one unity.

We have now learned to recognise the emotions, dispositions, and volitional processes as psychical contents, all of which differ from each other in their characteristic processes. None of them, however, contain anywhere specific elements. They can all of them be analysed into the same forms of feelings. Although the volitional process in especial is very peculiar, yet this peculiarity nowhere depends upon specific ideational or affective elements, but solely upon the mode of combination of these elements into emotions with their end stages again composed merely of general affective forms. Still there remains another question to be answered, which has not yet been settled by the reduction of all feelings to the above-mentioned six principal forms, viz. pleasure, displeasure, strain, relaxation, excitation, and quiescence. Is each of these forms perfectly uniform? Does it always return in the same quality? Or does it stand in a similar relation as the colour "blue" stands to the different shades of that colour, so that the principal form may not only appear in different grades of intensity, but also in various qualities? To answer these questions let us turn again to our metronome. It has again the advantage of illustrating our problem by means of a very simple example. Let us take two rows of beats in $\frac{4}{4}$ time with the accents arranged differently as in A and B, obtained by the method of subjective rhythm as described above.

A B

Both contain the same number of rises and falls, but in a different arrangement. A shows a pronounced example of a descending row of beats, B a similar example of a row that first ascends and then descends. With a suitable rapidity of the metronome we can easily hear at will into the uniform beats of the pendulum each of these rhythms. If, however, we have once made our choice between the two forms, then we group the beats that follow the row A in exactly the same manner as the row A, and the same thing happens with the row B. Such a spontaneous repetition is only possible owing to the fact that at the last beat of each row we group the whole together. This we do with the succeeding beats as well, just as we have seen to be generally the case in measuring the scope of consciousness. Now if we observe our feelings we obtain an important addition to our previous observations. They showed us that a very important part of such a process was composed of the alternating feelings of strain and relaxation, and perhaps also of excitation and quiescence, and lastly of agreeableness. This last feeling was especially strong at the end of a row of beats, caused by the arrangement of the single element into one rhythmically ordered whole. It is obvious now that the centre of gravity of the affective process lies every time at the end of a row, where the superimposed rhythmical feelings run together into one unity. For it is unmistakably this feeling that allows us directly to apprehend the succeeding rows as identical with the preceding ones in a succession of similar rows. What we apperceive is not the preceding row itself. The greater number of its elements lie already in the darker field of consciousness. We apperceive rather this aggregate feeling, which is joined to the last directly apperceived element, and which is the resultant of the preceding affective processes. Now let us compare this terminal feeling, that lends a given rhythm its essential and peculiar affective character, as it appears in the two examples represented by A and B. It is evident that however much on the one hand a row may depend upon the constitution and the arrangement of the preceding components, it yet on the other hand always possesses its own specific quality. It is true that we can always classify this under one or more of the six chief qualities, and yet we do not thereby account for its own peculiar quality, which differentiates it from the others of the same class. It also cannot be considered a mere summation of the simple feelings that are joined to the separate parts of the process. The feelings of strain and relaxation that are distributed over the rows A and B are the same. They differ at most in the degree of intensity. We cannot therefore understand why the feelings that remain behind at the end of each row should be so different. But it is so. We can convince ourselves of this more directly than in the experiments with voluntary rhythmical emphasis, if we produce the rows A and B after one another by means of knocking and without a metronome. Here the emphasised beats are not only subjectively, but also objectively accentuated. If, by this method, another observer compares the rows A and B given successively, he obtains at the end of each row such differing impressions that he cannot decide with certainty whether the rows are of equal or of different lengths. We saw above, that with the repetition of similar rows of beats, five rows of $\frac{4}{4}$ time could be apprehended at once. Now, however, as soon as the rhythm is changed, it is impossible to compare one single row with another of differing rhythm. The aggregate feeling concentrated at the end of each row of beats possesses each time a qualitative colouring dependent upon the constitution of the rhythm. This colouring coincides in its general form with the feeling of agreeableness that arises at the end and with the feeling of relaxation following the strain of expectation. These observations supplement essentially our former results as to the apprehension of longer rows of beats. We found that the knowledge that two rows were the same, always came at the end of a row, and that this verification followed the rows directly in one uniform act of apperception. Now we can explain this phenomenon perfectly by the uniform nature and the instantaneous rise of that resulting aggregate feeling. Because of this the last beat in a rhythmical row comes to represent the whole row. The quality of the rhythmical feeling that corresponds to the time in question concentrates itself in a perfectly adequate manner in the apperception. Thus the qualitative shades of feeling that are bound to the idea come to represent the idea itself. This substitution is of the greatest importance, above all from the fact, as we have clearly seen in the rhythmical experiments, that the ideas and their components lying in the darker fields of consciousness influence in their apperceptive affective power the process of consciousness.

What has been here explained with the simple example of a row of beats, can now be applied to ideational content of every kind. If we form a melody by combining the rhythm with a certain ordered change of tones, and if it is repeated, exactly the same process takes place as with the repetition of an unmelodious row of beats. The qualitative resultant of this whole, which here again is concentrated on the apperception of the last impression and which makes an immediate repetition possible, has, however, become very much richer. Here in the terminal feeling, preparing itself during the course of the melodious collection of tones, the whole concentrates itself again to a perfectly uniform affective product complete in itself. It is the very same with any other ideational compound. Even although the affective value is very weak, it always receives a qualitative colouring from the composition of the idea. This colouring appears, where other more lively affective reactions are wanting, as a modification of the delicate feelings of strain and excitation which accompany all processes of consciousness, and especially of apperception. The great importance which feelings have for all the processes of consciousness is often overlooked. This applies to the processes of memory, cognition and recognition, and also to the so-called activities of imagination and understanding. We shall return to this when we discuss these various forms of psychical combinations. At this point let us emphasise once again the result that our observations have led us to as to the real nature of feeling. We have called the feelings states that were connected with the subject, subjective reactions of consciousness. We see now that this description is not exactly incorrect, but that it is inadequate. What gives its psychical value to a feeling arising from any objective content of consciousness is not its connection with consciousness, but the fact that it is closely bound up with the apperceptive processes. Feeling is always bound to an apperceptive act. This came plainly to light in the rhythmical experiments where the feeling arose from preceding impressions. Feeling may therefore be looked upon as the specific way in which the apperception reacts upon the content of consciousness that stands in connection with the immediately apperceived impression.

Lastly, two other questions present themselves. How is it that feeling possesses the characteristic of appearing in certain contrasts, viz. pleasure and displeasure, &c.? And how is it that just three such pairs of contrasts exist, which we shall call for the sake of shortness the three dimensions of feeling? Since we are here dealing with ultimate facts of psychological experience, which cannot be further analysed, the answers to our questions cannot in the proper sense give an explanation of these facts. That is, in reality, as impossible as to explain why a blue colour is blue and a red one red. Considering, however, the connection of the feelings with the total processes of consciousness, we can try to explain these contrasts in this connection. The view of feeling as a way of reaction of the apperception upon a given content gives us some help in understanding these affective contrasts. We found that the act of apperception represented a simple volitional act.

Now each volition contains latently either an attracting or an opposing element. Our volition is attracted by the desired object, and it turns away from the one that opposes us. Herein lies expressed, as we can see, that fundamental relation of affective contrasts which now spreads into different directions in the basal forms of feeling. Among these the pair of contrasts of pleasure and displeasure may be looked upon as a modification of the attracting and opposing elements, which are directly connected with the qualitative constitution of the impression or the idea. What we desire is joined with pleasure, what opposes us with displeasure. On the other hand, the pair of contrasts of excitation and quiescence will very likely stand in direct relation to the intensity with which apperception enters into action, even although qualitatively the content that calls it into action be pleasurable, or the reverse, or indifferent. Now in so far as this action, called forth by a certain content, consists of an increase or decrease of the normal function of apperception, so the intensive side of the reaction divides up into these two opposites

—excitation and quiescence. Lastly, because of the relation between the successive processes of consciousness, each act of apperception stands at the same time in connection with the preceding and the succeeding processes. Now, according as apperception is directed to an immediately passed or to an immediately coming row, a feeling of relaxation or of strain arises. We may therefore look upon each single feeling in principle as a compound that can be divided up into all these dimensions and into their two principal directions. In each feeling these components are emphasised more or less strongly or are quite wanting, while all the time the total qualitative constitution of the content of consciousness gives to the whole its specific colouring, which distinguishes it from every other content.

# CHAPTER III

## ASSOCIATION

THE elements of our consciousness, as the foregoing discussion has taught us, stand in general combinations with each other. Even where objective impressions lack steady combinations, we are accustomed to construct such by means of subjective sensations and feelings. The single beats of a row on the metronome are as such isolated, but we combine them into a rhythmical whole by means of our feelings of strain and relaxation, and by means of weak accompanying muscle-sensations. We have seen that in this way the different ideational compounds, the complex feelings, the emotions, and the volitional processes are all resultants of the psychical processes of combination. Now, how are these combinations constituted, and what laws are they subject to? Psychologists generally have called them "Associations," since the English philosophy of the eighteenth century turned its attention to the importance of this process of combination. The opinion has often been expressed that this one concept is sufficient to include under it all psychical processes of combination. We shall soon see, however, that thereby a very important and characteristic difference is left out of account. We shall choose this difference, since it certainly influences all processes of consciousness, as our chief principle in a division of these combinations. This distinctive characteristic consists in the fact that one set of psychical combinations acts of its own accord, *i.e.* without the accompaniment of those feelings of activity which we learnt were constituent parts of the processes of apperception and volition; whereas another set is closely connected with these activities. At the same time, further distinctive characteristics in the combination processes run parallel to this one. Let us therefore call only those generally passive combination processes associations, and the active ones apperceptive combinations, or for shortness apperceptions. If we limit in this way the concept "association" in contradistinction to the ordinary use of the term, still we must enlarge it considerably on the other side, if we wish to do justice to all the combinations of this sort that really exist. The old theory of association was founded exclusively on the observation of the memory-processes. With such a process we are accustomed to take note, first of all, merely of the ideational compounds of consciousness, and secondly, the ideas in such a schematic memory-process are arranged regularly in a temporal succession; for example, an outward impression acts first of all upon consciousness, and then we remember something previous that was similar to this impression, or stood in relation to it. Now these memory-processes, as a closer inspection will show, make up a remarkably small part of our associations. They are in fact of much less importance than many other forms. As soon as we compare this form with other forms, we recognise at once that it is merely a secondary form.

If we wish to arrange associations according to their simplicity and the closeness of their combinations, we can start with the following simple experiment. If we make the string of a piano sound by plucking it in the middle, then, as the science of physics teaches us, not only does the whole string vibrate, but each half vibrates as well in a smaller degree, and in general each third part, each fourth, &c., in ever decreasing amplitudes. These segments, which decrease in length according to the numerical series 1, 2, 3, &c., correspond to tones of increasing pitch—the half string corresponds to the octave, the third part to the fifth of the octave, the fourth to the double octave, and so on. If these high tones are then produced alone, one after another, by making the corresponding part of the string vibrate each time, and if we then return to the tone of the whole string, we can then, if we listen attentively, hear clearly, along with the stronger sounding fundamental tone, these overtones, or at least those nearest to the fundamental. We therefore say that the clang of a string, or of any other musical source, does not only consist of the one tone according to which we determine its pitch, but also of a series of overtones, which give it its timbre or clang-colour. This expression itself points to the fact that in hearing a clang there takes place psychologically an association, which is of a specially intimate kind. The above-described experiment of comparing a clang with some of its overtones teaches us that these latter really exist in sensation, and that we can perceive them with very intense attention. Nevertheless under ordinary circumstances we do not perceive them as independent tones, but they appear to us massed together only as a specific modification of the fundamental tone, and we call this its clang-colour or timbre. An association of this kind, in which the sensation-components are so fused into the resulting product that they can no longer be clearly perceived as isolated component parts, is called a fusion. Such a fusion can be either a very close one or a very loose one. A single clang is for example a close fusion, a chord is a loose one. The separate fundamental tones of a chord are bound fairly closely into one whole, but we can hear at least some of them quite plainly.

Similar fusions occur in the various senses, and they become very complicated owing to the fact that sensation-elements of several senses are joined together at the same time. The disappearance of the components into one resulting product brings it about that we cannot directly perceive the separate elements that make up this product by means of direct sensation, as is in part possible in the case of clang-fusions. We are forced to make use of an indirect method. We proceed from the principle, that each sensation, a change in which is of essential influence on the resulting idea, belongs to the components of this idea. A pronounced case of this kind is seen very clearly in spatial ideas of the senses of touch and sight. If any part of the skin is touched with a little rod, we can, as is well known, with a fair degree of certainty apprehend the place touched, without looking at it. Now in the pathological cases of partial paralysis, it is shown that there are two kinds of sensations that are of essential influence on this localisation. Firstly, it is considerably disturbed by a partial suspension of the outer cutaneous sensitivity. In this case the patient often localises the impression on a place far removed from the place touched. Secondly, complete or partial paralysis of the muscles in the region of the place touched, *e.g.* the muscles of the arm and hand in the case of a touch sensation on the hand, causes just as much confusion in localisation. In this case as well the patient may localise the impression on an absolutely wrong part of the body. Therefore we must presuppose that neither cutaneous nor muscle sensations alone are the original cause of the idea of the place touched, but that both together by fusion give rise to this idea. After this has once happened, the quality of the touch sensation which is peculiar to each part of the skin and which varies with the place of the impression, can in itself bring about a localisation. That in general both components, *i.e.* cutaneous and movement sensations, must fuse together in order to produce an idea of a certain place or locality, is clearly shown in blind people, and especially in those born blind. In their case the sense of sight, which determines the whole perception of space for those who can see, is wanting, and we observe in them a continuous and very lively co-operation of cutaneous sensations and movements of touch.

Exactly corresponding to these relations in the sense of touch are the phenomena that we observe in the formation of visual spatial ideas. Here as well we notice two sensation-components regularly working together. The one consists of the sensations of the retina. Analogous to the touch sensations of the skin, they vary in quality not only according to the constitution of the outer impressions, but also according to the part of the retina which is affected by the impression. The other component consists of the extremely delicate sensations which accompany the positions and movements of the eye. They vary in their intensity according to the length of the distance through which the movement travels, just like the sensations of movement of the other muscles of the body. We notice, therefore, that changes in the position of the retinal elements, which may occur in inflammations of the inside of the eye, or abnormalities in the mechanism of the eye-movements may disturb considerably our spatial perception. They cause sometimes apparent dislocations in the objects seen, and at other times illusions as to their size and distance. These influences can be demonstrated on the normal eye by means of experiments. By making the movement of the eye more difficult, we cause the length of a distance to be overvalued. If we compare two straight lines of exactly the same length, one of which is interrupted by a number of transverse lines, so that a continuous movement of the eye is hindered, then this divided line appears longer than the undivided one. We can also by systematic experiments change the normal relation between eye-movements and retinal sensations. It will then be observed that our vision slowly begins to adapt itself to this new relation between the eye-movements and the position of the retinal elements. This can be done by wearing spectacles with prismatic glasses for a considerable length of time. At first all objects appear distorted. A straight line appears curved, a circle looks like an oval, and so on. If the spectacles are worn for several days, these distortions disappear. It may happen that distortions again appear when the glasses are discarded. This phenomenon can scarcely be accounted for except in the following manner. The retinal sensations by means of local differences in quality, which we may call qualitative local signs, correspond to definite sensations of movement graduated as to intensity, which we may call intensive local signs. Their relation to the centre of the retina probably determines this correspondence. Now our experiment with the prismatic glasses shows that this relation is neither an absolutely permanent nor an innate one, but that it is acquired by practice. It is acquired by the function itself, and therefore, when the functional relations are changed, gives way to a different relation or correspondence. This combination possesses distinctly the character of an association, and in so far as in it the sensation-components only appear as modified elements of the resulting spatial idea, it also possesses the characteristics of a fusion. In contradistinction, however, to the intensive fusions of clangs and chords, this possesses the special characteristic, that it consists of elements out of different senses. For the qualitative local signs belong to the sense of sight or to the sense of touch if we are dealing with spatial cutaneous perceptions which are exactly analogous to visual perceptions; whereas the intensive local signs belong to sensations of movement or muscle sensations. Both together form a complex system of local signs.

Just as sensations fuse together into more or less complex ideas, so also do feelings fuse together into complex compounds, in which single elements appear to bear the rest, which act in a modifying manner upon the form, something analogous to the overtones of a clang. These affective fusions are again bound up most closely with the ideational fusions that correspond to them. The impression of a musical chord is composed of both. Only in a psychological analysis can we separate the ideational from the affective associations, which are the essential causes of the æsthetic character of the chord. One of the most important and simplest affective fusions of this kind is that of the so-called "common or organic feeling." It consists of an indefinite number of organic feelings, to which more or less lively feelings are joined, which in this case pre-eminently belong to the class of pleasant-unpleasant feelings. In this case, just as in the case of a chord, certain elements are predominant, while the others are merely modifying concomitants. Our general state of health, *e.g.* freshness and activeness or general displeasure and exhaustion, is essentially a product of this affective complex, in which under normal conditions the sensuous feelings joined to the strain and movement sensations of the muscles play the most important part.

A most important form of fusion consists of the impressions of our sense of hearing and of our organs of locomotion. These impressions are the intermediaries of our ideas of time. If we divide up into their elements the processes of consciousness caused by metronome beats of a medium rapidity, we find two classes—those that belong to the class of sensations and those that belong to feelings. As sensations we have first of all the single metronome beats divided from each other by empty intervals. These are not the only sensations. As we have shown above, there is also a weak sensation of strain which probably arises from the tensor muscle of the tympanum, and which lasts continuously from one beat to the other. To this is joined a further sensation in the mimic muscles surrounding the ear. The whole process, therefore, looked at from the point of view of sensation, appears as a continuous sensation-process, which is interrupted at regular intervals by stronger impulses arising from the objective impressions of the beats. To all this, however, as we saw before, there is added the regularly alternating feelings of strain and relaxation, which determine the rhythmical ideas. All these elements of sensation and feeling form in reality an indivisible whole. If a temporal idea is to arise, none of these components may be wanting. If the sensations are wanting, the feelings have, so to speak, no foundation. They can only arise if sensation impressions are present, upon which the feelings of expectation and realisation can be founded. On the other hand the sensations remain unconnected, they lack a combination into a successive row, if the feelings of strain and relaxation are not present, for they directly help in the apprehension of the equality or inequality of the successive periods of time. If the beats are allowed to follow each other so slowly that the last one disappears out of the scope of consciousness when the new one enters, then the idea of time becomes absolutely uncertain. The same thing happens if, on the other hand, the time is so rapid that feelings of strain and relaxation cannot arise. In both cases it is obvious that any uncertain idea of time is only possible by reason of other extraneous factors. Just as all our objective measures of time, from the course of the sun to the vibrations of a tuning-fork used to measure time, depend upon regular periodic movements, so also is our subjective time-consciousness absolutely dependent upon rhythmical ideas. These arise first of all from our movements of locomotion, and then in a much richer and finer form are transmitted to us by our sense of hearing. In all these cases, however, the resulting idea of time can be divided up into a substratum of sensation and into an affective process of strain and relaxation, of expectation and realisation. In the idea of time they fuse perfectly together, so that the influence of these factors can only be shown by the essential changes, which the resulting idea undergoes, if one of these sensation or affective factors is altered in some marked degree.

Just as elements of consciousness are joined together by fusion into compounds, so these compounds themselves undergo manifold changes, out of which new combinations arise. Of great importance among these associations of the second class are those which we shall call assimilations and dissimilations. As ideational combinations they can be easily demonstrated, whereas the corresponding affective associations are joined to them rather as secondary components or form a special class of complex feelings, which are connected with the processes of recollection, recognition, memory, &c., and which we shall treat of in detail later on.

Let us first of all glance at some of the most important phenomena in connection with assimilation and dissimilation. To begin with the simplest case, we let one object of sight work in an assimilating manner upon another. We can achieve this most readily if we first of all make the difference between the two objects very small, and if secondly we bring them into a familiar relationship to each other, and so promote the idea of their identity. For example, we draw from one and the same centre sectors of a circle, and make one less than the others only by a few degrees. In spite of this we are inclined to apprehend all the sectors as equal. The larger ones work assimilatively upon the smaller one. To cause the opposite process of dissimilation, we draw one large sector among several smaller sectors. This appears, in contrast to the surrounding smaller sectors, very much enlarged, and we can convince ourselves of this by drawing on another piece of paper a sector of the same size as the one changed by dissimilation. This independent sector will then appear smaller than the one of its own size that is lying among the smaller sectors. This dissimilative change is generally called a contrast. We must not, however, confuse this dissimilative contrast with the contrast of feelings, where it is not a case of the formation of apparent differences in size, but of qualitative contrasts, such as pleasure and displeasure, or the increase of these.

More important than the assimilations and dissimilations between directly given impressions are those that arise out of the reciprocal action of a direct impression and of ideational elements, which belong to previous impressions, and therefore arise by means of an act of memory. Reproductive assimilations of this kind we have already met with in our reading experiments (see p. 26). We saw there that a well-known word can in general be read almost instantaneously, although its scope greatly exceeds that of the focus of attention. It is clear that this great facilitation in apprehension is only possible owing to the familiarity of the object, because by its action it gives rise to the reproduction of former corresponding impressions, and thereby causes the completion of the image only partially perceived. We can convince ourselves of this in a striking manner by means of reading experiments, in which certain letters of a fairly long word have been voluntarily altered. Such changes are then in general only partially or not at all perceived in these quick reading experiments. It may easily happen that we take the following combination of letters "Miscaldoniousness" for the word "Miscellaneousness," although four out of the seventeen letters of the word have been changed. If by chance our attention is very strongly concentrated upon one of the wrong letters, we can perceive the mistake, but for the other wrong letters the right ones are as a rule substituted. It is obvious that this phenomenon is exactly the same as the one we continually meet with when we overlook misprints in a book, only that in our experiments a false reading is greatly favoured by the shortness of the exposition-time. In all these cases we generally take it for granted that it is nothing more nor less than an inaccurate apprehension, as the expression "overlook" suggests. Yet our rapid reading experiments convince us that this expression is really incorrect. In reality it is not a mere not-seeing of the wrong letters, but a seeing of the right ones in the place of the wrong ones. If we call into our mind directly after the experiment the image we have seen, we can see very often in those very places, where a wrong letter stands, the right letter in the full distinctness of an immediate impression. This is, of course, only possible if the wrong letter is displaced by the reproduction of the right one. Such a process is obviously made up of two parts—firstly, the displacement of the wrong letter, and secondly, the reproduction of the right one. Naturally both acts take place quite simultaneously, and therefore we may look upon the displacement as an effect of the reproduction. In this combination of the two acts an assimilation process and a dissimilation process are joined together. By means of an assimilation caused by the other letters the right letter is reproduced, and this together with all the rest of the word has a dissimilating effect upon the wrong letter. At the same time a further conclusion follows from these phenomena, which is of importance for the understanding of all the processes of association. It is impossible to imagine that a combination of letters, such as we have given above, could work as a whole, and then, because it was wrong, be replaced by the right word. It is on the contrary obvious that processes of assimilation and displacement have only occurred at certain places. It is also difficult to take for granted that the observer has ever seen the word printed in exactly the same size and type as employed in the reading experiments. It cannot, therefore, be a single definite word-image that he calls to memory, but there must be an indefinite number of similar word-images, which affect assimilatively the given impression, and cast it into the word-form which we ultimately apprehend. From this it follows that these associations do not by any means consist of a combination of complex ideas, but of a combination of ideational elements, which may possibly belong to very different ideas. With this we see that assimilation is at the same time closely connected with the associations by fusion considered above. In both cases the association is an elementary process. The difference between the two forms consists only in the fact that the elements in a fusion are constituent parts of a complex impression, whereas in an assimilation they already belong to complex ideas, from which they then break away in order to enter into new ideational compounds. Thus fusion and assimilation work together in all sense-perceptions. The moment we see an object, hear a musical chord, &c., not only do the parts of the impression itself fuse together, but the impression also immediately gives rise to reproductive elements, which fill up any gaps in it, and arrange it among the ideas familiar to us. These processes continually overlap each other, and extend over all the regions of sense. What we imagine we perceive directly, really belongs in a great extent to our memory of innumerable previous impressions, and we are not aware of a separation between what is directly given us and what is supplied by assimilation. Only when the reproductive elements attain to such a striking ascendancy, that they come into an irreconcilable contradiction with our usual perceptions, are we accustomed to speak of a deception of the senses or of an illusion. But this is only a limiting case, and it goes over by unnoticeable intermediate gradations into normal associations, which we might just as well call "normal illusions." Many words of a leçture are imperfectly heard; the contours of a drawing or painting are only imperfectly represented in our eye. In spite of this we notice none of the gaps. That does not happen because we perceive the things inaccurately, as this phenomenon is often incorrectly interpreted, but because we have at our disposal the rich stores of memory, which fill out and perfect the perceived image.

This complementary association is met with in a striking manner, when a real assimilation is hindered by the associated elements belonging to different senses. In this case the difference in sense-quality erects, as it were, a partition-wall, which prevents the unobservable union of the elements. But at the same time even then close combinations can be formed, which at the operation of a sense-impression immediately reproduce the associated sensations of another sense. For example, we often observe in silent reading weak clang-images of the words, to which are joined slight movements of the articulation-organs, or at least indications of such movements. At the sight of a musical instrument we often perceive in ourselves a weak auditory sensation of its clang; the sight of a gun will often give rise to a weak sound sensation, or if we hear the gun fired, to a reproduced visual image, and so forth. Such associations of disparate senses are called complications. They form an important supplement to the associations, since together with these they essentially determine the ideational process in consciousness.

Such a co-operation of assimilations and complications is seen in the most striking manner in those processes of association which in ordinary life are called "recognitions," or, if the scope of the region of association over which the recognition stretches is indefinitely larger, are called "cognitions." We recognise, for example, an acquaintance, whom we have not seen for a long time. We know a table as a table, although we may never have seen the particular table in question before. We can do this by means of the indefinite number of associations with other tables, which the image of the table in question gives rise to. From what we have said above, it is at once obvious that all such recognitions or cognitions are nothing more than assimilations. The usual expression (to know or to be cognisant of) must not tempt us to look upon the process as a logical process, as an act of "knowledge." An act of knowledge may possibly follow a process of pure associative assimilation, if we afterwards try to account for the motives of the same. But the processes themselves, as they continually occur and make up an important part of our sense-experience, are pure associations. To place in them any acts of judgment or of reflection, as is customary in the scholastic psychology of ancient and modern times, can only serve to disguise the real psychological character of these processes. Among the associations called recognitions, only those are of special interest in which the consummation of the assimilation process is in any way hindered, either because the perceived object has but seldom been met with, or because it has undergone changes since a previous perception of it. For example it may, as is well known, take a long time before we recognise a friend, who meets us unexpectedly after many years' absence. If we observe the process in such a case a little more closely, it appears regularly that the impression of the individual which we first of all receive, appears to change because of certain lineaments, that are apperceived by means of our feelings, rather than brought into connection with the personality in question. Thus there arises a feeling of being acquainted with him, and then there occurs a second act, the real recognition, which follows in some cases very rapidly. This is the consummation of the assimilation proper. Here we see assimilation has turned into successive association, and we generally call it a process of memory. In fact this obviously arises out of an ordinary simultaneous assimilation, if the latter is hindered by some disturbing factor, so that the first impression and the assimilation of this impression form two successive acts. Such a dividing up into a succession generally occurs very distinctly, especially when the factors hindering the assimilation are so strong that it requires the addition of a further helping factor in order to overcome the hindrance. How often does it happen that some one greets us and we do not recognise him! If, however, he comes forward and mentions his name, suddenly the whole personality as a well-known one rises up in front of us. The reproductive assimilations are only set into motion by the addition of a helping idea. At the same time this example shows us how, in the dividing up of an assimilation process into a memory process, a complication may occasionally intervene. The name and the visual image are joined together as a complication, although in regard to the impression of human personalities in general they form fairly strong associations.

In these processes of hindrance and assistance of associations, which are to be observed in recognitions, feelings play a not unimportant part. We have indicated this already. In the above example, before we recognised the friend we had not seen for a long time, the act of recognition was prepared for by an indefinite kind of feeling, which with a certain suddenness, experiencing at the same time a noticeable increase in intensity, changed into the real act of recognition. How are we to explain this feeling? Whence does it come, and how can we explain its transition into the assimilation? The term a "feeling of familiarity" or a "quality of familiarity" with a thing has been used and has been regarded as a name for a specific element common to all acts of recognition. This was supposed to be affixed to every known object as a kind of outward sign. But the supposition of such an abstract symbol contradicts absolutely our observation. For, however indefinite this feeling may be in the period that prepares for the assimilation, it nevertheless possesses in each separate case its own peculiar quality, which is quite dependent upon the constitution of the recognised object. For example, the feeling differs, if we recognise an old friend, and if we recognise a district through which we have once wandered long ago. And it is by no means the same when we meet our friend Mr. X., and when we meet Mr. Y. whom we did not wish to see again. Just as much as the objects themselves differ, so do the so-called "qualities of familiarity" diverge from each other. From this we must conclude that these qualities are integral parts of the objects, naturally not of their objective nature, but of their effect upon us, or, more precisely expressed, of our apperception. Now we have learnt that the essence of feeling was just this influence of the ideational content of consciousness upon the apperception. It follows therefore incontestably, that this quality of familiarity is nothing more than the feeling character, which the recognised idea possesses for us. Now this feeling of being acquainted with a thing, as the above-mentioned observations teach us, may be very strong, while the assimilation of the new idea by the old is taking place not quite unhindered. We must therefore conclude that, in the period of preparation for the recognition, the assimilating previous idea is already beginning to make its appearance in the darker region of consciousness, and that it causes its corresponding affective reaction, but that it cannot itself force its way through to apperception. This interpretation of the process obviously receives fundamental support from our previous observations of the rhythmical feelings. With them it was also a case of recognition. If we repeat two similar rows of beats one after the other, we recognise the second as similar to the first. Now this can only happen, as we have convinced ourselves, if the total feeling concentrates itself upon the last beat of each row, which in its specific feeling-quality corresponds to the previous rhythmical whole. Exactly the same thing that happened in these rhythmical experiments, repeats itself now in these retarded recognitions of ordinary experience, except that in a way the distribution of the feelings is reversed. In the recognition of a rhythm the feeling corresponding to it arises out of the influence of the elements, that have receded out of the focus of attention into the darker field of consciousness, upon the apperception; in the steady rise of an impression to a state of recognition, the feeling is caused by the influence of the elements that are already in the darker field of consciousness but have not yet entered into the focus of attention.

In these complex processes of the recognition of objects, a further condition is added, which in the repetition of rows of beats did not make itself felt, at least not in the same degree, because of the simplicity of the phenomenon. It consists in the fact that each idea possesses a background of other ideas that are joined to it in a spatial or temporal connection, and that in the process of recognition these ideas may hinder or assist the assimilation process. They may retard the recognition or make it absolutely impossible, or they may form essential aids to it. Such secondary ideas can be observed very distinctly in cases where they join the chief idea after some time has elapsed. So in the above example, where the mentioning of the man's name caused a sudden recognition of the person himself; or, to take the reverse of this example, where the assimilation that is being formed is retarded owing to the fact that the name is other than the one suited to the motives of assimilation. Such secondary ideas are of course always present, even although we do not notice them. Even although they are in the darkest region of consciousness, they form, along with the feeling-tone of the chief idea, important components of the feelings accompanying the processes of cognition and recognition, especially in regard to their influence upon the apperception. In this way these latter are in reality always resultants of a sum of influences, and thus each separate experience, because of the unlimited variation of the secondary ideas accompanying assimilations and recognitions, possesses its specific feeling-tone, which distinguishes it from other previous or succeeding experiences.

Many phenomena that belong here escape ordinary observation, because their continuous repetition makes us insensitive to them. In those cases where an impression was accompanied by a very strong feeling-tone, and where its return is accompanied by a totally different affective state, we notice distinctly how the original feeling-tone becomes modified owing to the changed background. Thus every psychical process possesses its specific tone, even if it appears as a mere repetition of a previous process. The changing secondary ideas, by means of their own affective influences, give it its special temporal and local signs. By means of these each single process can be distinguished from any other, however similar this may be. The opposite phenomenon may also occur. Who does not know the strange feeling which occasionally comes over us at some process, the feeling that we have already in the past experienced this thing, although we know with certainty that this is in reality impossible? These phenomena also belong to the department of feelings, and we must connect them with the influences which arise from the indistinct secondary ideas, and which may at times almost exactly correspond, even when the chief ideas themselves are absolutely different. If such feelings become particularly strong, they very likely exert a reactive influence upon the assimilation process, and thus cause the new experience to appear as the repetition of a previous one. It may be that the so-called "second sight," which some people imagine they possess, depends upon very strong individual affective reactions of this kind and their assimilative influences. The ever-changing constellations of secondary ideas give each single experience its specific feeling-tone, by means of which it is distinguished from previous and following experiences. So it may happen that similar constellations of the darkly perceived content return in processes that otherwise are different, *i.e.* in the components that stand in the focus of consciousness. There is also another experience that may be mentioned here—one that has certainly escaped no keen observer of his own psychical life. If one calls to mind any previous experience, or in general any previous period of life—*e.g.* any definite period of one's childhood, of one's student life, or the beginning of one's professional career, &c.—each such striking experience or each such period of life is connected with a peculiar feeling, which also in this case enters into a distinct reciprocal action with the recalled ideas, inasmuch as it raises them to a greater degree of clearness and is itself increased by them. Any single recalled idea could scarcely account for the unusual intensity and the specific quality which these feeling-tones often reach. We must also remember that a clearly apperceived content in such cases seldom arises, and that in the second set (the periods of life) we have not as a rule one single idea. We can understand such cases by considering the fact that, if fewer definite ideas clearly arise, a great number of indistinct secondary ideas are active, and, since they are peculiar to each experience and to each period of life, call up again the corresponding total feeling, where a more definite reproduction of single ideas is absolutely wanting.

Let us return after this digression to the processes of recognition. The activity of the secondary ideas, that came to light in the experiences described above, helps us to understand some special characteristics that we met with in ordinary recognition, and still more so in the hindrances that this may experience. Especially in acts of recognition that are in some way or other retarded, we can in general observe a strong affective reaction arising, which, wherever we can bring it into connection with special motives, points to the effect of secondary ideas. They are as a rule only indistinct in consciousness, but sometimes they are afterwards recognised and prove themselves to be the motive, not only of the specific accompanying feeling, but also of the recognition itself. With these are closely connected other phenomena, which arise under circumstances where a real act of recognition never takes place, or under circumstances where the process, which is at first taking place absolutely within the region of the affective influences of the indistinct content of consciousness, more or less suddenly changes at most into an act of memory. A few examples will make such cases clear. Who has not had the experience of being for hours at a time oppressed with the feeling that he has forgotten something, or missed something, or done something wrong, without being able to explain what it is that oppresses him in this manner? Or who has not had experiences such as the following? I leave my house, and the moment I walk along the street I feel there is something I have forgotten; then by chance I pass a pillar-box, and it suddenly strikes me that I have forgotten to take with me an important letter. To such examples also belongs the torture we sometimes endure in trying to recall a name well-known to us. In such cases it often happens that we voluntarily try to obtain similar aids to our memory, as sometimes play a part in the retarded recognition of an individual known to us. Attempts have been made to explain all such cases by speaking of "states of consciousness"—an expression that tells us nothing and gives us no information as to the nature of these phenomena themselves. Now these feelings of forgetting, of thinking over a thing, of missing a thing, &c., are by no means always the same. They depend in each single case upon the special constitution of the idea in question. We can, therefore, in a manner analogous to our recognition experiments, interpret them as affective reactions to indistinct ideational content, in which the affective quality is dependent upon the specific constitution of the ideas, whereas the general affective character in the above-mentioned cases mostly belongs to the directions of strain and excitation.

The phenomena of recognition in their origin could be represented as simultaneous assimilations with occasional intervening complications. In their inhibition-forms, which we have just discussed, they lead us directly over to memory-associations. The old theory of association derived from these its schematism of association forms. In reality they are the association phenomena that are most of all noticed, because with them the ideas that are bound together seem to be distinguishable from each other because of their succession in time. Our previous discussion has, however, shown us that they are neither the only combinations of this class, nor even the most important ones. In fact they may be defined in accordance with their psychological origin as assimilations and complications, in which the combination of the constituent components is hindered by opposing motives, so that these components appear as independent ideas. This is seen clearly in such cases in which a continuous transition from the direct assimilative recognition, that takes place in a single act, to a memory-association is possible. Let us take, for example, the case of looking at a portrait of a well-known person, and let us imagine the portrait executed in the most differing grades of likeness to the original.

In the very rare cases, in which the painter achieves the greatest degree of likeness, it can happen that the picture gives rise to a very strong impression of identity with the original. There then arises a direct assimilation, which follows without any hindrance or retardation. If the picture is fairly good, so that the person may be recognised without any difficulty, but nevertheless possesses some strange lineaments, the process is one of retarded assimilation. The false parts of the portrait are after a longer inspection pushed aside by reproductive assimilation, and it may also happen after some time, that we see into this less excellent picture also the known personality. But if in the third and last case the portrait is much too unlike, there arises a peculiar competition between assimilation and dissimilation, in which it sometimes happens that we try to call up the memory-image of the person independently of the portrait we are looking at. It is usual to call this process "association by similarity," and to take for granted that the seen and the reproduced picture have been successively in consciousness. This is, as can easily be seen, a one-sided way of looking at the process; it is an attempt to make up a scheme out of an occasionally secondary phenomenon, whereas the essential part of the process, the competition between the assimilative and dissimilative influences, is quite overlooked.

There is yet another occasion, in which the assimilation of an impression may be analysed into a succession of ideas. This happens if the impression has been a component of a compound idea in previous experiences. The separate parts of this compound idea have been arranged in a succession, and this row itself may either be a temporal or a spatial one, and, in order to go through it, a succession of acts of apprehension are necessary. Both cases, temporal and spatial, are in essence identical, since they coincide as to the factor of succession. For example, if the words "I am the Lord" are seen or heard, then any one who is familiar with the Ten Commandments will feel inclined to continue, "thy God," &c., and this continuation may appear to him in visual word-images, or in weak sound-images, or the words may arise in the memory in complications made up out of impressions of both senses. It is usual to call this process "association by contiguity." Here also it is taken for granted that the directly impressed and the reproduced members of the row have joined together in pure succession. But this is also an imaginary scheme that does not correspond to reality. If we pay special attention to the course of the process, we clearly observe that the unseen or unheard part of the row does not by any means only enter consciousness, when the directly perceived part has already disappeared out of our apperception. We have rather in this case a phenomenon quite similar to the one we observed in the course of a row of beats or, in the reverse order, in the retarded recognition of an object. In the moment in which in the above example the word "Lord" was apperceived, already the whole succeeding content of the Decalogue was in the dark region of consciousness, so that from this the feeling-character, not only of the next words, but of the whole Ten Commandments, immediately conditioned the apperception. In reality, therefore, we have also in this case to do with a reproductive assimilation, in which the parts are apperceived successively because of the temporal arrangement of these parts, which are in reciprocal assimilation with each other. Just in the same way do the separate beats of a rhythmical row form a succession and still are at the same time a united whole in consciousness. This process becomes in a way modified, if an impression calls up memory-elements of different kinds, by which it can be assimilated according to the individual disposition of consciousness. If, for example, I hear the word "father" without any special connection with other ideas, I may according to circumstances bring the word "mother" or "house" or "land," &c., into assimilative combination with it. In such cases it may happen that a competition between these different reproductions may arise, similar to the one we observed in the examination of a bad portrait, and this is generally shown in feelings of displeasure and excitation, as also in a retardation of the whole process. But such phenomena seldom occur under the normal conditions of psychical life, although they form the rule in the so-called association experiments.

Our observations have therefore made it clear that the division, which to some extent still exists in present-day psychology, of all memory-associations into "combinations by similarity" and "by contiguity," rests upon a schematisation of these processes, in which their essential content, and in particular their close connection with simultaneous assimilations, remains unnoticed. The deeper reason for this method of observation, that operates more with fictions and formulæ than with real phenomena, may be looked for in the false materialisation of ideas. This has been consolidated rather than abolished by the conventional association psychology. A more thorough analysis of associations should have tended to abolish such a materialisation. The memory-associations were looked upon as the typical and only forms of association, instead of being considered as mere limiting cases, which are only developed under certain conditions out of processes of fusion, assimilation, and complication. The succession of two independent ideas, only joined together by outward similarity or by habitual contiguity, was made the basis for a scheme for all psychical processes. And thus the view was formed that each idea was an unchangeable thing, very similar to the object from which it arose. If we take an unprejudiced view of the processes of consciousness, free from all the so-called association rules and theories, we see at once that an idea is no more an even relatively constant thing than is a feeling or emotion or volitional process. There exist only changing and transient ideational processes; there are no permanent ideas that return again and disappear again. In the ideational processes there is a continual interaction among the elements out of which they are formed. A remembered idea is therefore as little identical with the previous memory-act of the same idea as with the original impression with which it is connected. Just as ideas are not permanent objects, so they are not processes that take place independent of feelings and emotions, for the more indistinct ideational content of consciousness by means of its feeling-tone influences apperception. From these again arise other combinations, which join together into one whole a number of contents of consciousness which belong together. Even with memory associations it is therefore never the complex ideas themselves which associate together, but each association divides up into a number of more elementary combinations. In these there are always processes of hindrance and retardation at work, so that the associated idea, in contradistinction to the original idea, of which it seems the renewal, can always show further changes, which depend upon the special conditions of their origin. Here those assimilations and dissimilations, which continually intervene as reproductive factors in our immediate sense-perceptions, make up the fundamental forms of the process, which determine all acts of memory. And these themselves can always be reduced to assimilation processes, which have been divided up into a succession, partly because of hindrances, and partly because of the temporal arrangement of the ideational processes themselves.

## CHAPTER IV

### APPERCEPTION

THERE are cases of severe insanity in which the patients utter with great rapidity a number of words, joined together without sense and sometimes intermingled with absolutely meaningless sounds. This symptom is considered a component of the so-called "flight of ideas." A sane person can also produce this, if he, without any train of thought, simply repeats any words that may occur to him. For example, the following is such a series of words: "school house garden build stones ground hard soft long see harvest rain move pain." Compare with this a context like the following out of the seventh book of Goethe's *Wilhelm Meister*: "Spring had come in all its glory. A spring thunderstorm, that had been threatening the whole day long, passed angrily over the hills. The rain-clouds swept over the land, the sun came out again in his majesty, and the glorious rainbow appeared against the grey background." Wherein do these two word-combinations differ from each other? We are perhaps inclined to answer that the first series is lacking in any connection between the separate elements. It seems almost like a series of words taken at haphazard out of a dictionary and placed aimlessly one after the other. And yet one soon notices that the separate words are not quite so unconnected, as at the first glance they seem to be. As a rule it is obviously some memory-association that combines the succeeding word with the preceding one, as "house" with "school," and "garden" with "house," and so on. Sometimes the association may join a word with one preceding it at a greater distance back, or it may join two different words to the same one, *e.g.* "stones" with "build" and "house," "ground" with "garden." Sometimes also it may not be the ideational content itself, but the mere rhyme, that brings about the combination, as with "rain" and "pain." In other cases we may not be able to find a definite association at all. And yet, considering the many-sided and darkly perceived ideas often caused by mere affective influences, which we have considered above, we cannot help taking for granted latent associations in such cases as well, and especially since these cases happen very seldom. A "free, unconnected chain of ideas," as is sometimes presupposed, we shall place at once in the same category with "chance" in the region of physical phenomena. Just as in the latter case, it simply means for us that the cause cannot be found in the case in question. From this point of view the first series of words is in some way or other psychologically conditioned in each of its elements by association, and still the series does not form a whole. It resembles in a way a heap of stones, out of which a house or several houses could possibly be built, but to make them into a whole the building plan, the unifying thought, is wanting. Now if we look at the second series of words, we see at once that in this case also the different parts are joined together by association. The general ideas of spring, thunderstorm, hills, rain, sun, and rainbow are all links in an association-chain. But these elements are so arranged as to make a unified image. The impression of this image places us at once in the situation and mood that the author wishes to awaken in the reader. In this picture none of the chief component parts are superfluous; each is in close connection with the whole, which as a total idea binds all these associated elements together.

Now if we wished to distinguish the second from the first of the above ideational series by the objective characteristic of the sensible arrangement of its separate components, it would not be possible in consequence of the subjective nature of the process. Let us suppose that a child learns by heart the sentences from *Wilhelm Meister* without in the least paying attention to the meaning of the words, as it occasionally may happen, then the reproduction of these sentences has for the child no sense. The difference between this and the first series as to its psychological character is only apparent and not real. The separate words in both cases are joined to each other by mere association. In the consciousness of the child they do not form a unified whole. Wherein lies the difference between this mere apparent unity of sentences learned senselessly by heart and the real unity in the mind of the author, who wrote them, or of the intelligent reader, who reproduces the picture in his mind? Let us try to answer this question in detail. The author who first formed the picture, and the reader who reproduces it, do not behave psychologically in exactly the same manner. The whole, even although in indistinct outlines, must be present in the consciousness of the author, before he writes down his sentences. He behaves, to take an example from our metronome experiments, in the same way as we do in listening to a certain rhythm, which we are hearing into the uniform beats of the metronome, or again, as we do when we beat with our finger a certain predetermined rhythm. The whole was in his consciousness, but the separate parts entered successively into the fixation-point of apperception and then ultimately ended at the end of the paragraph with the total feeling joined to the whole, which even at the beginning prepared for and influenced the coming paragraph. The state of the reader, who reproduces the author's thoughts, is a little different. From the beginning his attention is directed towards one total idea made up of many components, but this total idea is only produced from the impression of the words read. With the author the whole is there at the beginning and at the end of the production of the thought, which is itself developed in the successive apperceptions of the separate parts. With the reader there is at first only an expectation directed towards a whole. This expectation is shown in feelings of strain which are mostly regulated into definite qualitative directions, and these feelings are sufficient to guide the conception of the developing parts of the image into clear consciousness in the way in which the author himself raised his total idea, which was at first indistinct. Thus in both cases the activity of apperception is the essential factor, which makes a difference in the formation of such a combination from that of a mere association row. The thought-context changes into a mere association, if the separate parts of the same are joined together by memory alone and if they are reproduced without the inner unity of thought. Now such a reproduction becomes a passively experienced process, which lacks the consciousness of activity peculiar to the self-production of a thought and also, with the above-mentioned modifications, to its reproduction in the mind of the hearer or reader. In both these cases it is that feeling of activity, that we have mentioned above as the characteristic of active apperception, made up of alternating feelings of excitation, strain, and relaxation—it is this feeling of activity which gives the process the character whereby it differs essentially from mere association.

While all apperceptions agree in the objective characteristics of the combination of a complex into a unity and in the subjective one of voluntary activity, yet in a further comparison of our thought processes we meet with a very evident difference in the content of the combined ideas. Think, for example, of a sentence such as the following one from Kant: "Whether the treatment of knowledge, that belongs to a critique of reason, is proceeding along the sure way of science or not, can easily be judged by the result." If we compare this sentence out of the *Critique of Pure Reason* with the above description out of *Wilhelm Meister*, may we not be inclined to say that each belongs to quite a different world of thought? In our first example everything is graphic, each word represents a sensuous idea, the whole is a picture in words. In Kant not one single word is the expression of a concrete object, they are all abstract concepts, which only obtain some living content by means of further processes of thought, which they stimulate. And yet the abstract thought-compound corresponds with the concrete description in so far as it can be reduced ultimately to concrete concepts. It has to make use of words, which as impressions of the senses of hearing and seeing are themselves sensuous ideas. Certainly such concepts as "knowledge," "reason," "science," and even "treatment," "way," "result," which make up the sentence out of Kant, are not in the least of a concrete character in the way they are used. But if we go back to the original meanings of all these words, we find every time that it is a sensuous one, *i.e.* relates to the senses. "Treatment" at an earlier stage of language means something that we can treat in a material sense, "knowledge" refers to sensuous knowledge —something that we know by means of our senses, "reason" is nothing but the understanding of words or similar sensible impressions. As regards "way" it clearly bears the stamp of a concrete concept, it can be used as synonymous with "road." And yet in all these cases, the words in the thought, which they here help to express, are far removed from their origins. Thus the most abstract thought can ultimately be reduced in all its components to concrete concepts. And these words, the means of expression, which we cannot dispense with, at the same time bear witness to the fact that abstract thinking has developed itself step by step from concrete. The history of knowledge teaches us that this happened in the following manner. The original sensuous ideas entered into the most manifest relations with each other, and then just as at the primitive stage of thought the concrete ideas themselves were joined together as separate elements of one thought, so at a higher stage these relations between ideas were then treated as elements. So the word "knowledge" represents an almost unlimited number of processes of objective knowing, and thereby it becomes an abstract concept, which can no longer be directly considered concrete. In this way there is brought about, by an unceasing concatenation of apperceptions, a continuous concentration of the thought process, which at the same time represents a great saving and concentration in the work of thinking. A concept, such as "knowledge," is like a bank-note that represents an inexhaustible value of current coin. Very appropriate in this connection is what Mephistopheles says to the student in *Faust*, "One throw of the shuttle stirs up a thousand combinations." And even although with the help of this development in meaning of word-ideas the process of thinking may have very greatly diverged from its original sensuous basis, it nevertheless remains in the actual process always sensuous and concrete. For, to continue with Mephistopheles, "just where concepts are lacking, a word comes in at the right moment." Only in our sense the "word" has quite a serious meaning. The word is the real ideational equivalent for the concept, that cannot be formed into an idea. It changes abstract thoughts into concrete ideational processes that can be heard and seen.

By the side of these concentrations caused by continuous apperceptions, the primitive concrete thinking, along with all the intermediate steps between the concrete object and the abstract concept, always preserves its own value peculiar to each of these steps. And among this row of values it is the most primitive one, the one that is directed solely to the apprehension of reality, that receives a favoured place in our life and thought—in our life, since we belong to the immediate reality and intervene in it in our activity; in our thought, since we always must think the abstract thought-complexes made real in their separate applications, if we do not wish to lose ourselves altogether. The special value of primitive apprehension, unweakened by any kind of abstraction, finds expression in the fact that the two divisions of human mental activity, which as complements to each other make up the chief value of human life, *i.e.* science and art, make real the two forms of thinking. Hence the creations of art are no less thought-compounds than those of science. They follow in the general laws of their construction exactly the same laws of apperception, which we observed in the productions of thought contained in speech. The thought is as a whole in our consciousness, and at first only works upon the apperception by means of the resulting total feeling, and then develops into its separate component parts by successive acts of apperception. In exactly the same way the artist, the poet, or the composer is accustomed to grasp the whole of the work of art in its outlines, sometimes very indistinct, before he begins to carry out any of the parts, and while carrying them out a total idea is formed, which in its turn has a reciprocal influence upon the original idea. In both cases, especially through the influence of intervening associations, the thought-process or the composition of the work of art may undergo deviations or additions in its separate parts. The regularity of the process as a whole remains undisturbed by this. A work of art is just as little a mere product of association as is a thought arranged in sentences.

Various phenomena of everyday experience find their explanation in these psychological observations. First of all must be mentioned the seldom-noted fact, that we are able in our speech to bring to an end a fairly complicated thought without difficulty, although at the beginning of the sentences we are not at all clear as to the separate words and ideas or their combinations. Some people, when they are obliged to speak in public, fail simply because their confidence in this self-regulation of the train of thoughts is lacking at such moments. And this again is due to the fact that they think they must first of all find the suitable transition from one word to the next. In free conversation they can carry to an end without a break the most complicated sentences, while in public their speech is hesitating and embarrassed, and they are every moment in danger of breaking down. In such a case absolute confidence in the possibility of expressing freely and involuntarily the thought in one's mind is the surest help to overcome these difficulties. Of course a sensible training will also help.

Let us call to mind the processes by means of which the beginning and end of an expression of thought are held together into one sentence or into several sentences joined together by the same thought. We note at once that the general content in its whole feeling-quality is already present as soon as the first word is spoken, while the ideas and the corresponding words are not clearly in consciousness beyond that first beginning. If the process continues without associative distractions and additions, by which, occasionally, parts that lie far from the original thought are added to it, then we notice at the same time that that beginning feeling corresponds perfectly with the terminal feeling that accompanies the termination of the spoken thought. This terminal feeling is generally at first much stronger than the initial feeling, but then it gradually goes over into the feeling-quality that is preparing the next thought. Now it is obvious at once that all these phenomena correspond in essentials with those we observed in our metronome experiments. In these experiments the conditions were much more simple and exact, so that they strengthen the more uncertain observations in ordinary reading and thinking.

More complicated than in ordinary speaking and thinking are the phenomena where the sequence of thought-processes stretches over vast creations of the mind. Very likely the whole of the idea hovers in the mind of the artist, who has received an inspiration for a work of art, or of the philosopher, who is filled with the conception of a complicated system of thought, before either of them carries it out. This anticipation can only be considered an indefinite total feeling, which points the direction for the continuation of the thoughts, and which becomes clearer itself during this continuation. At the same time, in such complicated cases the distracting influences increase in power continually, and accordingly continually alter the quality of the feeling-tone that hovers over the whole. So it sometimes happens that the resulting product becomes in its execution quite different from what it was in its first conception, and it sometimes may happen that such changes occur several times in the course of the process. In all such cases this is generally caused by new associations, which arise from single elements of the total thought, and which, if they do not fit into the regular course, often assimilate with the total thought in a similar manner, or crowd it out altogether. In combinations of creations of thought these secondary influences ultimately increase so much that the regular steady course becomes an exception, and the preponderance of these transforming forces becomes the rule. Although in most cases these phenomena defy objective control, yet there are examples enough in which they can be clearly seen, at least their broad outlines. So Goethe's *Faust* shows clearly traces of a repeated change in the idea of the whole, and the supposition is forced upon us that the author in his later conceptions had forgotten his first ones. In *Wilhelm Meister* it almost seems as if he purposely had given as much free scope as possible to the play of associations caused by the plot. These may be extreme cases, and yet there is hardly in the province of science or art any creation of thought which in its execution remains free from any such intervening influences, which have their source partly in new impressions and partly in the thought-compounds caused by the execution or the elaboration of the same in the mind. The two psychical processes, that here interact, have been brought by psychologists under the concepts of "understanding" and "imagination." Where a regular arrangement of the thought-compounds, bound up with a tendency to form them abstractly, is uppermost, it is the custom to assign this to the understanding. Where consciousness is more inclined to the free play of associations and of newly excited thought-forms, and at the same time to a more concrete form of thinking, it is customary to speak of the activity of the imagination. But really we are here not dealing with faculties of thought that can in any way be separated, not even with functions of a different kind, but at bottom always and only with a participation of the apperceptions and associations that enter into all processes of thought, though distributed in a relatively different manner. It is therefore an absolutely wrong conception, if, according to the tradition of the old psychology, imagination is called the specific property of art, and understanding that of science. Science without imagination is worth just as little as art without understanding.

These general conceptions of understanding and imagination correspond in a certain sense only to different points of view, under which we look at the mental functions, in themselves indivisible, and by means of which we separate them according to the relative participation of their factors. So in the same way associations and combinations of apperception are not processes which belong to differing regions of our psychical life. On the contrary, not only are they always in a state of interaction, but apperceptions show that they arise out of associations, wherever we are able to trace them back to the conditions of their development. Nowhere can we see so clearly this rise of apperceptive combinations out of association as in spoken thought, the region of mental activity which is more than any other open to us in its objective forms. Let us explain this by means of an example, which is closely connected with the above examples of concrete and abstract forms of thought. We have taken the sentences out of *Wilhelm Meister*, which describe the coming of spring, as a sample of sensuous objective expression in the sense of forms of thought-construction familiar to us. And yet they are absolutely controlled by the laws of our abstract thinking, which join together widely separated elements of thought to one total idea in the interests of a unified combination, and compel us to use, in the form of particles and inflections, abstract elements of conception in order to arrange the parts of the scene described. This is different at a more primitive stage of thinking and expression in speech. Let us take, for example, the following simple statement in our own language: "He gave the children the slate-pencil." This sentence is for us directly concrete. If, however, we were to translate it just as it stands into the language of the inhabitants of the African colony Togo, they would probably not understand it. For such an individual even "slate-pencil" would be too abstract a conception. Further, he would not be able to imagine how any one could give something without having first of all taken it from somewhere else. The elements inserted between "slate-pencil" and the action of giving, which to us serve to combine the whole into one single idea, would mean to him rather a mixture of disparate elements. Lastly, he cannot form the concept "children" without thinking that they are children of some people or other. Accordingly our sentence would run somewhat as follows in the speech of the Togo negro: "He take stone to write something this gives of somebody child they." We must note here that even this literal translation still bears traces of the abstract culture of our language. The difference between substantives and verbs, which we have been forced to use, does not exist in the Togo language. If we look at such a sentence a little more closely, it is at once evident that the ideas are arranged exactly in the same order in which the objective process takes place. Each word denotes only one idea and is not placed in any grammatical category, since there are none such in this language. Therefore the expression of thought is still in essentials at the stage of pure association of ideas. Such a sentence only differentiates itself from a perfectly unsystematic association, that strays from one member to the other — as in the above-mentioned series, "school house garden &c." — by the fact that it follows directly the action described element for element, and therefore reproduces this in the memory exactly as it took place in perception.

Here we meet clearly the two motives which raise pure associations to apperceptive combinations by means of the impulses that lie in the association itself. One of these motives is an objective one. It lies in the regular concatenation of the outward phenomena which present themselves to our view, and which force the association to combine the ideas in the same regularity. A series, such as "school house garden &c.," is only possible when the thought process frees itself from perception and gives itself up to the incidental inner motives, which remain when the continuous succession of phenomena that regulates our thinking is wanting. Therefore association that is joined to these phenomena is in itself the more primitive, and in this way it is the regularity of the course of nature, which transfers its regularity to the normal association of our ideas. Added to this objective motive there is a second, a subjective one. We would not be able to hold together in association a series of impressions given to us in a certain order and to reproduce them again, were it not for our attention that follows from member to member the separate parts of the series, and ultimately binds them together into a whole. Thus ordered thinking arises out of the ordered course of nature in which man finds himself, and this thinking is from the beginning nothing more than the subjective reproduction of the regularity according to law of natural phenomena. On the other hand, this reproduction is only possible by means of the will that controls the concatenation of ideas. Thus human thought, like the human being himself, is at the same time the product of nature and a creation of his own mental life, which in the human will finds that unity which binds together the unbounded manifoldness of mental contents into one whole. In this way the development of apperceptive thought-combinations out of associations corroborates further the result obtained above in considering volitional processes, namely that to every outward voluntary action there correspond inner acts of volition which are occupied in influencing the course of thought. In the close combination between thought and speech this connection between inner and outer volition comes most clearly to light. We cannot act outwardly without at the same time executing inner acts of will. Therefore ordered expression of thought in speech corresponds as outward volitional activity to the control of the will over the associations that originally stray here and there without order. Even although thought in a primitive speech, as in the above example, may be ever so near to mere association of ideas, yet the control by the will is also to be seen in it, from the fact that the association series is one that inwardly is connected together. And with this we have the basis upon which the more complicated forms of apperception can rise, because of the continuous concentrations and combinations in thinking, and these latter at the same time find their adequate expression in the forms of speech. This connection between inner and outer volition, as we see it living in the connection between thought and speech, is ultimately of as great practical as theoretical importance. Only by considering this connection do we arrive at a sufficient understanding for the higher productions of human mental life. It also points forcibly to the fact that the most important part of education for the formation of character—*i.e.* the training of the will—should not only, and not even in the first instance, be directed to the outward act. Rather must education pay most attention to that inner volition which is occupied with ordered thinking. To make this strong, to make this able to resist the distracting play of associations, is its most important and also one of its most difficult tasks.

Many attempts have been made to investigate the processes of thought in other ways than in the way described above. At first it was thought that the surest way would be to take as a foundation for the psychological analysis of the thought-processes the laws of logical thinking, as they had been laid down from the time of Aristotle by the science of logic. Scholastic philosophy showed great subtlety in this direction in changing psychical processes into logical judgments and conclusions, and there are still followers of this direction at the present day. Starting with the thought-processes in the narrow meaning of the word, this logical explanation of everything psychical was allowed to spread over to associations, the processes of sense-perception, the pure sensations, feelings, emotions, &c., so that in this old scholastic psychology the human consciousness was in danger of becoming a scholastic philosopher, who regulated each of his actions according to the laws of logic. Now such laws are a late product of scientific thinking, which presupposes a long history of thinking determined by a number of specific factors. These norms, even for the fully-developed consciousness, only apply to a small part of the thought-processes. Any attempt to explain, out of these norms, thought in the psychological sense of the word can only lead to an entanglement of the real facts in a net of logical reflections. We can in fact say of such attempts, that measured by results they have been absolutely fruitless. They have disregarded the psychical processes themselves, and have gained nothing at all for the interpretation of the laws of logic simply because they saw in them the primitive facts of consciousness itself.

Many psychologists thought that this method could be improved by making use of direct introspection. They thought by turning their attention to their own consciousness to be able to explain what happened when we were thinking. Or they sought to attain the same end by asking another person a question, by means of which certain processes of thought would be excited, and then by questioning the person about the introspection he had made. It is obvious to the reader, who has followed our discussion so far, that nothing can be discovered in such experiments, where the most complicated psychical processes are investigated directly and without any further preparation. We need first of all a careful analysis of the more elementary psychical processes, of the facts of attention and of the wider scope of consciousness as well as of the relations between them and of the manifold affective processes that intervene in all these cases. Without having gained by these means the necessary information as to the general conditions and, so to say, as to the scene over which our thought-processes move, it is impossible in any way to understand these themselves in their psychical combinations. Many psychologists have connected this difficulty, not with the wrongness of their own method but with the essence of the thought-process. This was explained as an unconscious and (since all sense-perception belongs to consciousness) as a supersensual phenomenon, in the interpretation of which each one must be left to his own speculation. This opened the door at once to the explanation of psychical phenomena according to logical reflections, that were at will read into such phenomena. This alleged method of exact introspection ended ultimately at the point from whence it started, *i.e.* the scholastic philosophy.

In contradistinction to all this let us remember the rule, valid for psychology as well as for any other science, that we cannot understand the complex phenomena, before we have become familiar with the simple ones, which presuppose the former. Now the general phenomena of the course of simple processes in consciousness, as we have seen them in their most concrete form and under the simplest conditions in our observations of the combination and comparison of rows of beats, give us the most general preliminary conditions, which must be held as a criterion for much more complicated thought-processes. It is evident, however, that these formal conditions of all processes of consciousness cannot be sufficient to account for the special characteristics and phenomena of the development of thought. To do this we must turn our attention to this development itself, as it is shown in the documents of the spoken expression of thought at different stages of consciousness. It is unfortunate that in these and in other cases the development of the child, that is for us the easiest to observe, can give, as is obvious, only a few and in part only doubtful results. The speech and thought of the child, under the present conditions of culture, not only presuppose a number of inherited dispositions, whose influences can scarcely be accurately traced, but it is also absolutely impossible to withdraw the child from the influences to which, from the very beginning, its environment gives rise. Therefore the mental development of our children is under all circumstances not only ar accelerated but also in many respects an essentially changed one, in comparison to a purely spontaneous development. On the other hand there are, at least in a relative manner, such stages of a spontaneous development of thinking, in many cases relatively independent of outward influences of culture, in the mental life of more primitive peoples. The different stages, which this mental life shows, find their most adequate expression in the outward phenomena of this mental life itself, and above all in those of speech, which is a means of expression and an instrument of thought at the same time. We can by means of the different stages of the development of speech follow that gradual transition of associative into apperceptive processes of consciousness from step to step. The example given above of a relatively primitive form of spoken thought shows the relation in which it stands to our languages of culture. A closer investigation of this subject would lead us beyond the scope of individual psychology into that of racial psychology, where the most important part deals with the psychological development of thought and speech.

# CHAPTER V

## THE LAWS OF PSYCHICAL LIFE

MANY psychologists and philosophers have denied the existence of special laws for our psychical life, if we understand this to mean specific laws, differing from the universal physical ones. Some say that everything that is called a psychical law is nothing but a psychological reflex of physical combinations, which is made up of sensations joined to certain central cerebral processes. Others maintain that there are no laws at all in the mental sphere. They say that the essential difference between natural and mental sciences consists in the fact that only the former can be reduced to definite laws, whereas the latter are absolutely wanting in any arrangement of phenomena according to law. The first of these opinions, that of materialistic psychology, can be passed over rapidly. It is contradicted by all the phenomena of consciousness that we have up till now discussed. It is contradicted by the fact of consciousness itself, which cannot possibly be derived from any physical qualities of material molecules or atoms. The indisputable affirmation, that there exist no processes of consciousness that are not in some manner or other connected with physical processes, is changed by this materialistic hypothesis into the dogma that the processes of consciousness themselves are in their real essence physical processes. Now this is an assertion that directly contradicts our immediate experience, which teaches us that a human being, or any other similar living creature, is a psycho-physical and not only a physical unity.

The second of the above opinions ascribes to the natural sciences alone laws in the sense of universally valid rules for phenomena, and therefore limits psychology in principle to the description of facts, which appear in their combinations to be arranged purely by chance or at will. This opinion rests obviously on a mistaken use of the conception of law. We are only allowed to consider those regularities in phenomena as according to law, which always repeat themselves in exactly the same manner. But there are in reality no such laws, not even in the natural sciences. For this principle is valid here: laws determine the course of phenomena only in so far as they are not annulled by other laws. Now because of the complex nature of all phenomena in general each process stands under the influence of many laws, and so it happens that just the most universal natural laws can never in experience be demonstrated in their full power. There is no law of dynamics which has a more universal validity than the so-called "law of inertia" or Newton's first law of motion. It can be formulated as follows: "A body in motion, and not acted on by any external force, will continue to move indefinitely in a straight line and with uniform velocity." It is obvious that this law can never and nowhere be realised in experience, since a case of independence from other external forces, which alter the motion, never and nowhere exists. And yet the law of inertia is for us an infallible law of nature, since all real processes of motion may be looked upon as lawful modifications of that ideal case (never existing in concrete experience) of a motion not acted upon by any external influences.

Let us now in the light of these considerations, universally acknowledged in natural science, consider the question of the existence or non-existence of psychical laws. It is of course self-evident that we may consider as laws only such regularities that lie within the process of consciousness, and not such as lie outside of consciousness, *e.g.* such as belong to physiological processes of the brain. Accordingly we may call combinations of sensations or of simple feelings into complex ideas, emotions, &c., psychical laws, if they in any way take place regularly. On the other hand, the fact that, if a bright point appears on a dark field of vision, the lines of vision of the two eyes are at once directed towards this point—this fact is a physiological and not a psychical law. Naturally such physical laws, as the one in our example, may have a determining influence upon the operation of certain psychical laws. But this does not hinder us from making a sharp distinction between the two kinds of law. We keep as a principle for a psychical law, that the components as well as the resultants of the effects of such laws are parts of immediate consciousness, *i.e.* sensations, feelings and their combinations. Now if we cast a glance, while keeping firmly to this criterion, over the manifold processes of consciousness, which have been touched upon in this book, we see at once that all these processes bear the character of a stern regularity. Not in the sense that these laws are fixed rules without exceptions (such laws as we have seen above do not exist, because of the never-failing interference from other influences), but in the only sense permissible, *i.e.* that each complex phenomenon can be reduced to a lawful co-operation of elements. If this requirement were not fulfilled, there would be no cohesion in our psychical life. It would break up into a chaos of unconnected elements, and consciousness itself, which is just the opposite of such a chaotic disarrangement, would be impossible. Therefore each separate idea is a combination of sensations according to law. A given clang of a definite timbre is put together unchangeably in the same way out of elementary tone-sensations. That certain objective sources of sound, *e.g.* strings, air spaces, possess physical qualities, by means of which such regular combinations of tone-quality arise, is undoubtedly a very important factor for the psychical law of the blending of tones. But these physical facts have in themselves nothing whatever to do with this law. If our consciousness was not disposed to such regular combinations, those objective factors would remain powerless. And it is exactly the same with the combination of light-sensations into spatial ideas, with the union of the images of an object in the right and left eye into one total image, with the rise of peculiar total feelings out of their partial feelings, as we have observed in the organic feeling and in the elementary æsthetic feelings, and last of all with the composition of the emotions and volitional processes out of their elements. Starting from these single more or less complex processes of consciousness, this character of regularity applies above all to the temporal succession of the processes. The generalisations of the old association psychology were absolutely inadequate, and its chief mistake lay, not so much in postulating laws too hastily, as in the fact that it did not attempt to penetrate deeply enough into the laws underlying the association processes by means of an analysis of the same. A last and conclusive testimony for this lawful character of psychical phenomena is given by the apperceptive combinations, whose specific products (of course quite dependent upon the laws of association), are the combinations of the thought-processes, as we have seen above. There can be no more striking proof of the absurdity of the above-mentioned theory of the lawlessness of psychical phenomena as the consequence to which it would lead us. For it would lead to the conclusion that the conception of law itself was contrary to law. This conception is in fact nothing more than one of the results of those psychical thought-combinations, the lawful nature of which is questioned.

It would lead us too far here to go into the profusion of psychical laws. The general character of them has been suggested in our chapters on association and apperception. In the natural sciences there are more general fundamental laws that rise above the separate particular laws, and these we may call the principles of investigation, in so far as they are general requirements to which investigation has to conform. In the same way we can set up fundamental laws in psychology which are not included in the separate regularities of phenomena, because they can only be gained from a general view of the whole of such phenomena. In physics, for example, the above-mentioned example of the law of inertia is a universally valid law. The same claim is raised in a wider scope by "the law of the indestructibility of matter," and by the near-related "principle of the conservation of energy." Are there, we naturally ask at once, psychological principles of similar universal validity?

Before we attempt to answer this question we must note one restriction, to which even in the natural sciences the requirement of universal validity for the leading principles is subject, and which, we may be sure, will be even more prominent in mental science, because of the extraordinarily complex nature of the phenomena. This restriction consists in the fact that the validity of each fundamental principle is subject to certain hypotheses, so that, where these are no longer fulfilled, the principles themselves become doubtful or untenable. Thus the law of the conservation of energy is only valid as long as the measured units of energy belong to a closed or finite material system. It loses its validity if the system is of infinite extent, or if, though finite, it can be acted upon by any external forces. A restriction analogous to this last one will have to be employed in regard to the psychical laws obtained by generalisation from the individual psychological regularities. Of course we must take into account the conditions arising out of the peculiarity of mental phenomena. These psychical laws, by virtue of the subjection of psychical phenomena to the interconnection of consciousness, can only be valid within the limits within which such an interconnection of psychical processes takes place. We shall, for example, try to obtain a fundamental principle which controls the formation of complex psychical processes out of their elements. But it would have no sense to set up such a law for absolutely disparate processes that do not stand in any relation in the single consciousness. It may be that, because of this, the limits of validity for psychological principles are much narrower than those for general natural laws. This is connected with the fact that psychology has to do with inner and not with outer relations. And also we must not forget that this limitation can be compensated for by the character of the psychical laws themselves. And, in fact, the discussion of the first and most general of these laws will show us that this hypothesis proves correct.

The first fundamental principle deals with the relation of the parts contained in a complex psychical process to the unified resultants into which they form. This relation can, as regards its qualitative content, be a most extraordinarily varying one, so that, in regard to the quality of the elements and their combinations, the separate psychical processes cannot be compared. Thus we cannot compare simple light sensations and qualities of tones, or a spatial visual image with a compound clang, or bring into comparison, according to their qualitative character, the relations of both of these pairs with those of the elements of an æsthetic feeling to that feeling itself, or with those of the separate feelings of an emotion to the total content of the same, or with those of the affective and ideational components of motives to the volitional process in which they take part. Nevertheless all these cases are regulated in regard to the formal relation between the components of a process and their resultants by one single principle, which we may call, for the sake of shortness, "the principle of creative resultants." It attempts to state the fact that in all psychical combinations the product is not a mere sum of the separate elements that compose such combinations, but that it represents a new creation. But at the same time, the general disposition of this product is formed by the elements, so that further components are not necessary for its creation, and indeed cannot be considered possible from the standpoint of a psychological interpretation. Thus in the light sensations of the retina, combined and fused with the sensations of strain in the eye in its movements and adjustments, are contained the essentials for the production of a given spatial image. At the same time this spatial image itself is something new, which as regards the resulting qualities is not contained in those elements. In the same way an act of volition that takes place under the influence of a number of motives, partly combating and partly aiding each other, is the necessary creation of this motivation, so that any specific process lying outside of these elements is nowhere to be observed. At the same time such an act of volition is no mere sum of motive-elements, but something new, that connects these elements into one united resultant. We see this creative and yet absolutely lawful nature of psychical phenomena best of all in apperceptive combinations, and for a long time it has been silently recognised in their case. Every one knows that the result of a chain of reasoning, made up of a row of single acts of thought, may be a product of those single thought-acts, which throws much light on some subject and which was before unknown to us, and yet which conclusively comes from those premises, if we analyse retrogressively its development. Upon this creative character of apperceptive combinations, above all, rests the regularity of psychical development, which is shown in the single consciousness during the individual life, and in the total mental development revealed to us by culture and history. The assertion that is occasionally made, based on dogmatic prejudices--namely, that the law of the constancy of matter, that is valid for the forces of nature, must necessarily keep mental life always at the same level in its total value—this assertion is contradicted by the facts of individual and universal development. That does not naturally exclude the possibility of individual interruptions of the course of development, and, because of these, of retrogressive movements arising, in consequence of the above-mentioned conditions, which govern all mental combinations. This combination of creative growth and strict regularity, which marks our mental life, is shown above all in the fact that, especially with the more complicated processes and the more extensive forms of progress of psychical phenomena, the future resultants can never be determined in advance; but that on the other hand it is possible, starting with the given resultants, to achieve, under favourable conditions, an exact deduction into the components. The psychologist, like the psychological historian, is a prophet with his eyes turned towards the past. He ought not only to be able to tell what has happened, but also what necessarily must have happened, according to the position of events. This point of view has in essentials for a long time been held in practice in the historical sciences. It must be of some value that psychology can show the same law of resultants even in the simplest sense-perceptions and affective-processes, where, in consequence of the simplicity of the conditions, very often the retrogressive deduction turns at the same time into a prophecy of events.

The law of resultants undergoes an important change in those cases, in which in the course of a psychical process secondary influences arise, which lie outside the region of the immediately produced resultants, and in which these secondary influences become independent conditions of new influences, which combine with those immediate resultants into a complex phenomenon. In such cases it may even happen that the secondary influences obtain the mastery and so degrade the original resultants to mere secondary influences or ultimately obliterate them altogether. Such a phenomenon may in longer processes be repeated several times and in this manner produce a chain of processes, the members of which diverge more and more from the starting-point of the row of phenomena. It is most of all processes made up of all other psychical compounds, *i.e.* volitional processes, in which this modification of the law of resultants may be demonstrated by means of numerous phenomena mostly belonging to racial psychology or the history of civilisation. An action arising from a given motive produces not only the ends latent in the motive, but also other, not directly purposed, influences. When these latter enter into consciousness and stir up feelings and impulses, they themselves become new motives, which either make the original act of volition more complicated, or they change it or substitute some other act for it. We may call this modification of the law of resultants, in accordance with the principal form in which it appears, "the principle of the heterogony of ends." It is of eminent importance for the development of the individual as well as of the general consciousness, and especially because the influences of original motives, that have decayed, are almost always preserved in some few traces alongside of the new ones that have taken their place. Such remnants of former purposes continue to exist in forms we do not understand in a great number of our habits, customs, and above all in religious ceremonies handed down to us from the past. Not only do these phenomena themselves remain obscure, but also the development of the present aims remains obscure, as long as we cannot account for them by the principle of heterogony that intervenes in all these cases.

As a supplement to the law of resultants, and yet at the same time in a certain sense as an expression for the same psychical regularity, we have "the law of conditioning relations." Just as the law of resultants joins into one unified expression the forms of psychical synthesis, so we may say that the law of relations is the analytic principle, which arranges under one general rule the relations of the components of one such synthetic whole. This rule consists in the fact that the psychical elements of a product stand in internal relations to each other, out of which the product itself necessarily arises, while at the same time the character of a new creation (a character that belongs to all psychical resultants) is caused by these relations. By inner relations we mean such as depend upon the qualitative constitution of the separate contents, and in so far stand, as a specifically different and at the same time complementary condition, in contradistinction to those external relations, which are determined by their formal arrangement. In this sense this distinction between external and internal relations corresponds to the difference in the ways of viewing the phenomena by the natural sciences and psychology respectively. The processes of nature are absolutely determined by the connection of temporal and spatial relations, in which the elements of the phenomena stand to each other. The mental processes on the other hand cannot, because of their subjection to natural phenomena, dispense with these external relations, but their inmost nature rests on the internal qualitative relations of the elements bound into one whole.

The law of relations stands in general reciprocal relationship to the law of resultants. Both of these laws apply to all compound unities of psychical phenomena, from the simplest ideational and complex affective processes up to the most complicated individual and general developments in psychical life. Thus the combination of a sum of tone elements into a single whole, by means of a specific ideational and affective value resulting from the combination itself, depends absolutely upon the qualitative and quantitative relations in which the tones stand to each other. This clearly arises from the natural dependence of resultants and relations upon each other, since each change of the latter modifies the constitution of the resultants in a corresponding manner. In the same way a spatial visual image is dependent on the relations of the qualitative and quantitative elements of the sensations of the retina and the strain sensations of the eye, and so on. A complex æsthetic feeling is a resultant of the simpler æsthetic feelings bound to the different parts of the perception, in so far as these latter again determine the product by means of their qualitative relations. And lastly all the processes of mental development are founded on the relations of their separate factors, by means of which they are combined into resultants. The interdependence of the laws of resultants and of relations shows us the importance of each of these principles. We cannot explain the psychical value of new creative compounds without considering the internal relations of their components, just as we cannot comprehend the peculiarity of these relations without continually taking into account their resulting influences.

Again in this case the most striking proof for the close connection between these two principles is given by the apperceptive combinations, especially in the forms of logical processes of thought, as they are expressed in the combination of sentences in speech. The thought-content of a sentence stands first of all, as we saw above, as a whole in our consciousness, but not yet as an ideational compound raised to clear apperception. In this stage it is a resultant from previous separate association and apperception processes. Then follows in the second stage of expression in speech, an analysis of that total idea into its parts, in which these parts are always put into close relations with each other. Such relations are called by grammarians subject and predicate, noun and adjective, verb and adverb, &c. The grammatical meaning of these categories shows clearly that this analysis consists of a system of primary and secondary relations, which are joined into a unified resultant by this logical arrangement. Thus the relation of subject and predicate includes all those further relations of noun and adjective, verb and object or adverb, as its minor terms, which are joined together partly by their own relations and partly by the relations of those most general members of the sentence, *i.e.* subject and predicate. This explains the psychological fact, that after this process of joining the thought together has passed, the total idea is once again, as at the beginning but this time more clearly, in consciousness. In a similar manner such single thought-compounds are combined into more extensive chains of thought, of which the relatively simplest forms are found in the process of drawing a conclusion.

The law of resultants finds a supplement and a specific application in the principle of the heterogony of ends in certain very important cases. In the same way we find, as supplementary to the law of relations, "the principle of intensifying contrasts." It includes those relations of psychical elements and compounds which are connected with certain limiting values of the qualitative and quantitative components of a whole. In the region of ideational combinations we have noted such influences of contrast in associative assimilations and dissimilations. We saw there that at a certain limiting value of the difference between two sensations or ideas, *e.g.* two spatial or temporal distances, two sound or light sensations, the assimilation present at a small difference may turn suddenly into a dissimilation. The impressions no longer assimilate, but become intensified through contrast. In another especially important form we meet the same principle in the feelings, where it stands in connection with the duality of the feelings that is valid for all affective processes and their combinations. In consequence of this each feeling, as we have seen, possesses its contrast-feeling, *e.g.* pleasure and displeasure, excitation and quiescence, strain and relaxation. Here the principle of relations shows itself in the form of the law of contrast, above all in the fact that the change between contrasting feelings itself intensifies the contrasts. Thus a feeling of pleasure is more intense, and its specific quality is more clearly felt, if it has been preceded by a feeling of displeasure. A similar relation exists between excitation and quiescence, strain and relaxation.

The law of contrasts is by no means limited to the relation between separate contents of consciousness existing side by side or following each other, but we see its most important influences in those places where it extends over more extensive groups of mental experience. Thoughtful historians have long since noted the fact, that in historical development not only do periods of rise and fall follow each other, but also periods of a special direction of mental life. And these periods, both in the impression they make upon us and in the objective relations in which they stand to each other, are so intensified that the following phase is every time increased by means of the contrast with the preceding one. Let us take an example from the near past. The German literature of the classicist period received its peculiar stamp of contemplative calm and beauty of form to a great degree from the contrast with the "storm and stress" period that was marked with such strong emotions. In the same way romanticism, which was inclined to the cult of the imagination and of a poetical past, was influenced by contrast with the preceding classical period, that laid most stress upon the understanding, and that regarded the present as the ripest fruit of human development. And lastly this change of contrasts shows itself most clearly and with the shortest oscillations in economic life, where it is in part assisted by the oscillations in the conditions of civilisation. We see this, for example, very well in the fluctuations of our national credit and of stocks and shares. And these sharp contrasts can be ultimately explained by the inner life of man that fluctuates between hope and hesitation, and in this fluctuation intensifies the emotions.

Let us now consider the connection of the four principles we have discussed. The second and fourth may be looked upon as special applications of the two fundamental principles of creative resultants and conditioning relations. We see also that they are not only joined very closely together, but that they stand, as absolutely disparate incomparable laws, in contradistinction to those general principles to which all natural phenomena are subjected. A contradiction has very often been thought to exist in the relation between the universal mental and natural laws. And since the natural laws are considered to be the more general and more necessary, these psychical principles have been looked upon as inadmissible generalisations, if they have not been absolutely ignored, which has more often been the case. Now we have seen in our whole discussion, that in reality we cannot move a step in the interpretation of psychical processes from the simplest sense-perceptions and affective combinations to the most complicated mental processes, as shown in society and history, without meeting with these principles always and everywhere. We must of course keep strictly to the maxim of analysing the psychical processes in their own connections and as processes joined together in themselves, as far as they so appear to us. Now the neglect of this maxim has led to the abovementioned contradiction and to the disregard of these laws. In fact the reverse maxim has been formed, namely, that psychical processes should not be held as decisive for the principles that condition them, but rather that the laws of nature, founded upon external natural phenomena, should also rule our mental life. In this sense the law of the conservation of energy has been considered a fundamental law of all mental development. For this purpose, and also in order to preserve a kind of independence for our mental life, the conception of "psychical energy" has been formed. This, in all the changes it undergoes, is supposed to be subject to the law of the conservation of energy just like mechanical, thermal, electro-magnetic, or any other energy. Since we do not possess a definite unit of measurement for this psychical energy, and since it always occurs between two other physical energies, it was taken for granted that it could be indirectly measured. It could be placed in the middle of a series of transformations that took place according to constant equivalents as a value to be measured indirectly by the physical energy equivalent to it. For example, it could be placed between a given quantity of chemical energy, supplied from outside to the organism, and an equivalent quantity of warmth and mechanical work-energy, which the organism produces. If this were the case we could not reconcile with it a principle such as the one of creative resultants. Such a principle could not be included among the universal psychical laws; it would have to lie outside the general regularity of our psychical life. We can of course reverse this relation. Then we come to the result, that psychical regularity lies outside the law of energy, and in that case it would have no sense to place this psychical energy between two other physical energies and then attempt a measurement. Such a measurement is a pure fiction. We might just as well take any other fictitious process, say a miracle, and place it in the series of transformations.

These applications of physical laws to psychical phenomena are not based upon empirical facts, but they arise from a metaphysical principle, namely, the demand for a monistic view of life. Now this idea certainly has a justification, inasmuch as it rests upon a logical demand which it seeks to satisfy. If the so-called monism does not do this, it changes into a real dualism, as would clearly happen in the above-suggested rationalistic explanation of a miracle. In fact monism is only scientifically justified in its view of the relation between psychical and physical, as long as it emphasises the fact that the human being can just as little be considered a purely physical as a purely psychical being, and that man must be considered a psycho-physical individual, as we in reality experience him. This monism alone corresponds to the facts. A dualistic separation of soul and body, even if it sails under a monistic flag in the form of an atom-soul, or of an anonymous psychical energy, is a hypothesis which cannot be proved and which is useless for the interpretation of mental life. From the standpoint of the scientific and only justifiable monism, the mental processes are considered inseparable components of human and animal life. They must be judged according to the qualities that are immanent in them, and not according to laws which apply to other phenomena, and in the formulation of which no regard was paid to those psychical qualities. There cannot, however, be the least contradiction in the idea that physical and psychical phenomena follow different laws, as long as these laws are not irreconcilable with the actual unity of the psycho-physical individual. In reality we cannot talk of irreconcilability in this case, because firstly, the two series of phenomena are of a disparate nature, and because secondly everywhere, where these two series of phenomena meet together in the unity of the individual, they are really, as far as we know, subject to a principle of regular arrangement. Thus, for example, the law of creative resultants is not the least contradiction to the law of the conservation of energy, because the measures by which we determine psychical values cannot be compared with those with which we measure physical values. We judge the psychical according to its qualitative value, and the physical according to its quantitative value. The idea of value is in its origin really psychical, and this points to the fact that in reality physical values have in themselves no real measure, and that they only obtain one, if we make them the object of a comparative judgment, *i.e.* in a sense translate them into the psychological. Disparate values cannot in any way be compared, so long as a transformation of the one into the other is impossible. We can compare warmth and mechanical work, because the one can be transformed into the other according to a strict law of equivalence. But we cannot compare a tone with a sensation of light, or a visual idea with a chord, because a transformation of the one of these practical contents into the other is unthinkable. Now physical values are subject to the principle of the conservation of energy because of the unlimited capacity for transformation of physical energies according to equivalent relations. But it has on the other hand no sense to try to apply this same principle to the qualitative psychical values, which do not in any way admit of such a transformation. This of course stands in close relation with the fact that the subject-matter of psychology is the whole manifoldness of qualitative contents directly presented to our experience, each of which would immediately lose its own peculiar quality, if we tried to transform it into any other. Thus the physical phenomena investigated by the natural sciences and the laws of these phenomena do not in the least contradict the qualitative content of life dealt with by psychology. They rather supplement each other, inasmuch as we must combine them together into one whole, if we wish to understand the life of the psycho-physical being given to us in its unity.

Yet this impossibility of comparison of these qualities could not exist along with the unity of their substratum, if the physical and psychical values were not joined together in this substratum. This connection consists herein, that on the one side the physical elements, whether atoms or parts of one continuous matter, must necessarily be thought by us in forms of spatial and temporal ideas arising in accordance with psychical laws, and on the other side the psychical elements, the simple sensations and feelings, are inalienably bound up with definite physical processes. These latter need by no means be of a simple constitution, as has at times been presupposed by reason of metaphysical prejudices. The opposite is rather the case, as experience, which alone in this question can decide, incontestably teaches. For it shows that each simple sensation is joined to a very complicated combination of peripheral and central nerve-processes, and so also with the most elementary feeling, as is shown by the manifold "expression" phenomena which accompany the simplest feeling.

The actual correlation then is between simple, *i.e.* not further analysable, psychical content and complex physical processes. If, however, in contradiction to this, we introduce the metaphysical postulate of a correspondence between the psychically simple and the physically simple, we are inclined to go further and to presuppose a continuous correspondence between the two series of phenomena right up to the highest and most complicated content of consciousness. This regular relation between psychical elements and physical processes then becomes changed into a metaphysical parallelism, in which in content as well as in form the psychical becomes a copy of the physical, and the physical a copy of the psychical phenomenon. This hypothesis finds expression in the words of Spinoza, "The order and combination of ideas is the same as the order and combination of things." Such an idea was thinkable as long as the physical side of the qualities of living beings was so little known, and as long as there was no explanation of those psychological principles, which control the combination of processes of consciousness from simple sense-perceptions to complex thought-processes. At that time philosophy could take the liberty of building up reality out of abstract ideas, such as substance and causality. At the present day metaphysics, if it wishes to make any claim to respect, must build upon the real facts and not upon those ideas used from purely logical, dialectical motives. Even from this point of view there remains a "principle of psychological parallelism" in the sense that there is no psychical process, from the simplest sensation and affective elements to the most complex thought-processes, which does not run parallel with a physical process. Now sensation and affective elements cannot be compared in that way, since a simple process in the one case does not correspond to even a relatively simple one in the other, and this of course is valid for all other contents of consciousness formed from these elements. We meet everywhere physical and psychical as incomparable qualities of the united psycho-physical individual, and each of these must be judged according to the laws of combinations of elements, which are expressed in the combination itself. Since these qualities themselves are disparate, it can therefore never happen that the two principles come into antagonism with each other, whereas on the other hand, if we try to transfer the conditions that are only valid for the one side of the phenomena of life to the other side, we will very soon either come into antagonism with facts, or be forced to abandon an interpretation of a part of life placed in this manner under a strange point of view. Thus from the present-day psychological standpoint, which must be authoritative for a philosophical consideration, we can only speak of a "parallelism" between psychical and physical in as far as all elements of psychical life are joined to physical processes. The combinations of these elements, however, can never be judged according to the laws that are valid for the combination of the physical processes of life. If we try to do this, we eliminate what is most characteristic and important in our mental life. This reduction of the so-called principle of parallelism is occasionally called inconsequent and unsatisfying. This objection rests upon the interference of *a priori* metaphysical theories of the past, whose principles have long been thrown aside by science, and also upon ignorance of the real problem which psychology has to solve. This problem can surely never consist in applying, in connection with psychical processes, principles which do not belong to the psychical side of life. It must much rather consist in the attempt to gain principles out of the contents of our psychical life, just as in the reverse case physiological investigation of the change of matter and energy in the organism does not in the least, and rightly so, trouble itself with the psychical qualities of the organism. For the real unity of life will not be understood by subjecting real phenomena to laws with which they have absolutely no inner relationship. No, we must try to explain all sides of life and then the relations of these to each other.

From the standpoints which have here been developed as to the relation of psychical to natural laws and as to their combination into one unity, we may now decide a question which is of mythological origin, and which was transferred by mythology to philosophy and ultimately to psychology. This question is the one as to the nature of the soul. For the primitive thinker the soul was a demoniacal being, which had its seat in the whole body, but especially in certain favoured organs, such as the heart, the kidneys, the liver, or the blood. Besides this oldest idea of a body-soul, there soon arose a second idea of a soul only externally bound to the parts of the body, and this soul left the body at death in the last breath, and also for a short time during sleep, as noticed in the images of dreams. This was called the breath-soul or the shadow-soul. For a long time, in spite of the self-contradiction, these two conceptions were joined together, although we see in the development of mythological thought that the breath-soul or psyche slowly supersedes the idea of a body-soul.

The development of the idea of a soul in philosophy is in essentials a repetition of this mythological development. The ancient philosophy, in whose footsteps mediæval philosophy follows, still holds fast to the idea of a body-soul. The soul is the driving force of all, even physical processes of life, *e.g.* nutrition and propagation. By the side of this, however, the higher mental activities are bound to a specific being that is separable from the body. This opinion, which gave a concrete, clear form to the mythological ideas, found its most perfect scientific expression in the psychology of Aristotle. The psyche that was separable from the body had thus won a victory over the body-soul both in mythology and in the classical work of Aristotle. This, of course, led ultimately to the absolute dominion of this independent soul, and its qualities were more and more considered to be absolutely opposite to the qualities of the body, that was ruled by purely material laws. This development culminated in the system of Descartes, the last great philosopher of the Renaissance. The body is from now on considered to be an extended substance, subject to mechanical laws only; the soul stands, in contradistinction to this, as an unextended, purely thinking substance. The two substances are, however, during life externally joined together. In one single point of the brain the body was supposed to meet in reciprocal action with the soul, which was thought of as something analogous to a material atom. Descartes fixed upon the pineal gland, but there were countless other hypotheses as to the position of this point.

This is not the place to follow the further changes that these ideas underwent in the history of modern philosophy and psychology. All the later changes of the dualistic hypothesis are not of the first importance. The fundamental principle is, that the soul is a permanent substance, and the psychical processes are looked upon as changing phenomena of this substance, which are, however, different from it. This hypothesis may take the form that Spinoza gave it in presupposing the two substances changed into two attributes which run parallel with each other. There is also the materialistic hypothesis that reduces the soul-substance to a quality of the bodily substance, which alone is recognised as real. It becomes clear to us that such further developments of the "substance" hypothesis become more and more contradictory to the laws of psychical life, the more they attempt to explain the self-contradicting conception of two absolutely different substances which must be bound together into one unity. The Cartesian soul can no longer exist in face of our present-day physiological knowledge of the physical substratum of our mental life. And metaphysical monism in these two forms, which try to combine soul- and body-substance into one unity, would shut out the possibility of any knowledge of our psychical life.

Therefore, in contradistinction to this metaphysical concept of a mind-substance, we set up the concept of the actuality of mind. Mental processes are not transient appearances to which the soul stands in contradistinction as a permanent, unknowable being unrelated to them, so that any attempt to combine the two must necessarily lead to a tissue of influences and counter-influences, which were at will given the conventional names: "ideas, feeling, striving, &c." A striking example of the futility of such an attempt to make substance the basis of an explanation of mental life is seen in the last and most thorough-going of these theories, *i.e.* in Herbart's so-called *Mechanism of Ideas.* Certainly all psychical phenomena is a continual coming and going, a producing and being produced. But no supersensuous substance, standing in contradistinction to these phenomena, can help us to understand the latter in their separate parts, or even in the connection of these parts into a whole. Sense-perception is a product of elements of pure sensation, an emotion is the course of directly experienced feelings, a thought-process is a combination of its elements established by itself. Nowhere do these facts of real mental life need another substratum for their interpretation beyond the one that is given in the facts themselves. And the unity of this life does not gain in the least, if we add to its own real union another substance, which is neither perceived nor really experienced, but which stands as an abstract conception in contradistinction to that mental life established by itself.

We only need to cast a glance at the sciences most closely connected with psychology, *i.e.* the so-called mental sciences, in order to become aware of the emptiness and futility of this psychological conception of "substance." The name "mental science" has only the right to exist, so long as these departments of learning are based upon the facts of psychology—the mental science in the most general sense of the term. Now when would a historian, philologist, or jurist make use of any other means to understand some phenomenon or of any other arguments to prove some statement than those which spring from immediate facts of mental life? Why then should the standpoint of psychology be in absolute contradiction to the standpoints of its most nearly related sciences? Psychology must not only strive to become a useful basis for the other mental sciences, but it must also turn again and again to the historical sciences, in order to obtain an understanding for the more highly developed mental processes. Racial psychology is the clearest proof of this latter. It is one of the newest of the mental sciences and depends absolutely on these relations between psychology and the historical sciences. It is the first transition from psychology to the other mental sciences.

The metaphysical psychology of the present day, that has developed out of Descartes' theory of two substances absolutely different and yet externally joined together, this psychology seems unquestionably to be further away from the reality of the mental life than the theories of the ancient metaphysicians were. The old idea saw in the soul the principle of all life, or, according to Aristotle, the energy working towards an end, out of which the whole of the phenomena of life, physical and psychical, sprang. It sought at least to account for that unity of life, which popular dualism must regard as a wonder, if it does not suppose the psychical to be a confused image of the physical, or reversely suppose this latter to be a mere subjective idea without its own reality. And yet this old vitalistic idea of a soul is for us no longer possible. For it tries to explain the unity of life only by postulating an all-embracing idea of purpose or use in place of a causal explanation of phenomena such as is now demanded. This vague notion of purpose does not explain the peculiarity of mental processes, nor does it fulfil the requirements of a natural explanation in regard to the physical side of the phenomena of life. Nutrition, propagation, movement, on the one hand, and perception, imagination, understanding, on the other, cannot be combined into one unity, even although the facts which these concepts denote are purposeful from the standpoint of the connection of the phenomena of life. They do not resist such a combination because they are bound up with essentially different substrata, but because they depend upon absolutely different standpoints of the phenomena of life given to us as a unity. Nutrition, propagation, movement, are organic processes which belong to objective nature, and for which, because of their own characteristics, the ideas we form of them serve as signs which point to an existence independent of our consciousness. In investigating them, just as in the investigation of natural phenomena outside our own body, we must abstract from the subjective processes of consciousness, to which they are bound, if we wish to understand them in their objective natural connection. On the other hand our ideas, inasmuch as they are subjective, our feelings and our emotions are immediate experiences, which psychology tries to understand exactly in the way in which they arise, continue, and enter into relations with each other in consciousness. Therefore it is one and the same psycho-physical individual forming a unity, which physiology and psychology have as subject-matter. Each of these, however, views this subject-matter from a different standpoint. Physiology regards it as an object of external nature, belonging to the system of physical-chemical processes, of which organic life consists. Psychology regards it as the system of our experiences in consciousness. Now for every piece of knowledge two factors are necessary—the subject who knows and the object thought about, independent of this subject. The investigation of the subject in his characteristics, as revealed to us in human consciousness, forms therefore not only a necessary supplement to the investigations of natural science, but it also attains to a more universal importance, since all mental values and their development arise from immediately experienced processes of consciousness, and therefore can alone be understood by means of these processes. And this is exactly what we mean by the principle of the actuality of mind.

THE END